LAS CAPILLAS DEL NORTE

Viewed across grassy fields—
Pinon-scented air rustles leaves
Fallen from nearby cottonwoods
Surrounding silent camposantos.
Monuments of ageless adobe
Stand majestically—
Double-thick walls echo
Voices of our ancestors—
Ceremony, prayer, rituals,
Scents, alabados—
Sunlight filters through
Dust laden windows .
Falling upon graceful altars
Adorned with century-old relics.

Marie Romero Cash, 1992

Built
of Earth
and Song

Built of Earth and Song

CHURCHES OF NORTHERN NEW MEXICO

Marie Romero Cash

Photography by Jack Parsons

RED CRANE BOOKS

Santa Fe

FIRST EDITION

Manufactured in Korea
Cover and text photographs by Jack Parsons
Cover photograph tinted by Jim Mafchir
Maps by Fred Cisneros
Design by Jim Mafchir

p. i, Church at Hernandez, N.M., ca. 1935. Photo by T. Harmon Parkhurst. Courtesy Museum of New Mexico, Neg. No. 11488.
p. ii, Church at Ojo Caliente, N.M., ca. 1890. Photo by Dana B. Chase. Courtesy Museum of New Mexico, Neg. No. 14408.
p. iv, Church interior, corbels and vigas, Santa Cruz, N.M., ca. 1912. Photo by Jesse L. Nusbaum. Courtesy Museum of New Mexico, Neg. No. 13921.

Library of Congress Cataloging-in-Publication Data

Cash, Marie Romero.
    Built of earth and song : churches of northern New Mexico / Marie Romero Cash. — 1st ed.
        p.   cm.
    Includes bibliographical references.
    ISBN 1-878610-30-9
    1. Adobe churches—New Mexico.   2. Church architecture—New
    Mexico.   I. Title.
NA5230.N6C37   1993   92-44089
726'.5'09789—dc20   CIP

Red Crane Books
826 Camino de Monte Rey
Santa Fe, New Mexico 87501

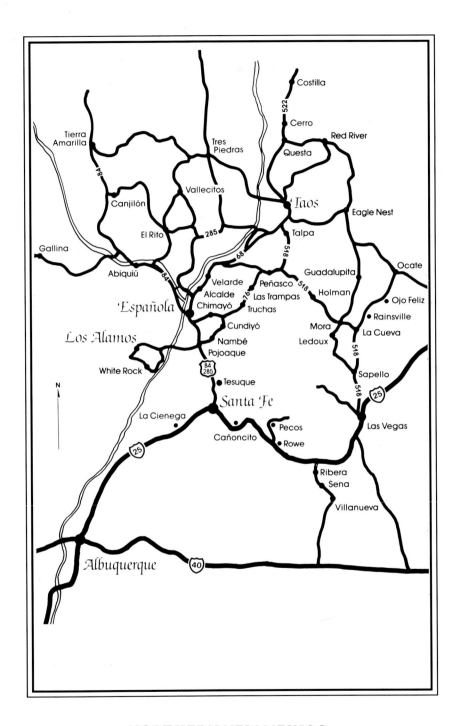

NORTHERN NEW MEXICO

CHURCH AT LAS TRAMPAS, N.M., ca. 1950

Photo by Tyler Dingee. Courtesy Museum of New Mexico, Neg. No. 73766.

CONTENTS

CHAPTER THREE
ALONG THE HIGH ROAD TO TAOS

CHAPTER FOUR
THE ABIQUIÚ AREA

CHAPTER FIVE
THE TAOS AREA

CHAPTER SIX
THE MORA AREA

CHAPTER SEVEN
THE PECOS AREA

APPENDIX: 155
THE CHURCHES OF NORTHERN NEW MEXICO
AND THEIR CONSTRUCTION DATES

FOREWORD

Much of a scholarly nature has been written concerning the religious architecture of New Mexico during the Spanish colonial era. Thanks to Eleanor B. Adams and Fray Angelico Chavez's superb translation and editing of the 1776 journal of the meticulous Franciscan *visitador* Fray Francisco Atanasio Domínguez, the detailed description of the eighteenth-century mission churches has been made available. John L. Kessell, in equally competent fashion, has brought the story of those edifices up to the present in *The Missions of New Mexico Since 1776*. There are other informative accounts of the early period.

Likewise, art scholars have focused on the statuary and other furnishings of the mission churches. Chief among these are the late E. Boyd's definitive studies of religious folk art, especially her identification of the *santeros* who fashioned the *retablos* and *bultos* and her discussion of their works. Fortunately, William Wroth, Donna Pierce, and Larry Frank among others, are continuing in that tradition.

These publications are classics in their own right. But important as their contributions are, they by no means tell the whole story of northern New Mexico houses of worship, for the missions are, after all, monuments to the colonial past. In addition, since then literally scores of religious buildings have been erected; some are sizeable, handsomely constructed, and well furnished, but many, especially those built in the last century, are small and unassuming, usually built by the parishioners themselves. But the creativity and tradition of the saint-makers have not been extinguished, for some of the later structures contain images fashioned by modern santeros, including the author of this book.

Until Marie Romero Cash undertook this study, no attempt had been made to inventory the extant churches and chapels of northern New Mexico and to chronicle their history. She has carefully incorporated the basic research concerning the colonial structures, but the emphasis is on the more modest later buildings, especially the little religious homes of the faithful. She makes no pretense to a scholarly approach, which indeed would be virtually impossible, even if it were desirable, since most of the information can come only from the local people themselves. Many of the simple churches stand in remote areas and even when seen by an occasional passerby are not unusual enough to attract attention. Some of the small settlements which they serve do not even appear on a map.

This warm, almost personal account is of special interest to those who travel northern New Mexico byways and to all who appreciate and wish to know more about the religious folkways of its people.

Myra Ellen Jenkins, Ph.D.
Santa Fe, New Mexico

PREFACE

My introduction to the churches of northern New Mexico came about quite by accident. When I was a child growing up in Santa Fe, my family never traveled much, and my meanderings were limited to a route between home, Saint Francis Parochial School, and Saint Francis Cathedral. As the years passed, the scope of my explorations was expanded to include Don Gaspar Avenue to Harrington Junior High School, and the plaza area on my way to Santa Fe High School. I grew up believing that most Spanish Catholic children led sheltered lives such as mine—centered around home, church, school, and the traditional food and music of the area. Since the age of six I had played the accordion for many local baptisms and weddings, accompanying my Uncle Willie, who played guitar, and another of his musician friends—all orchestrated by my father, Emilio Romero, who had always loved traditional Spanish music.

Many years later in the mid-1970s, while searching for my vocation, I turned to traditional Spanish folk art and began to produce my own renditions of the classic *santos*—*bultos* and *retablos*—housed at the Museum of International Folk Art in Santa Fe and featured in various publications. It was not until the early 1980s, however, that I became aware of the vast amount of historical data about regional churches that had not yet been researched.

At that time Father Jerome Martínez y Alire, then pastor of San Juan Nepomuceno Church in El Rito, approached me about the possibility of painting a massive altar screen for the 150th anniversary and rededication of the newly renovated church. This commission was the largest I had ever received. Although I was excited about the possibility, I had no clear idea about what building an altar screen involved; in fact, I had never seen one except in books. A few weeks later, Father Jerome took me on a tour of the northern New Mexico churches, a visitation that would have a profound impact on my life from that time on. Entering the churches at Córdova, Truchas, Las Trampas, and Picurís Pueblo, I was in complete awe. Never had I seen such splendor: the monumental altar screens; the santos, all dressed up in their exquisite handsewn clothes made by caring parishioners; the handmade tin frames and sconces. Of course, the splendor was not as dramatic as at the cathedrals in Mexico, but the architecture and artwork of these village churches had their own enchanting, hypnotic qualities. If only the walls could speak, to tell us of the origins of these images—what the *santeros* were like and how they felt, and about the care and faith which were the foundations of these wonderful churches, some built as early as 1776. My question then to Father Jerome was whether there was an inventory of all the pieces of historic artwork contained in these churches; he replied that there was not.

After I had completed the panels for the El Rito altar screen, they were placed in a framework built by my husband, Don Cash, and fastened to the 4-foot wall of the right-hand *crucero*, the front part of the church. The successful completion of this project brought many more commissions for altar screens from priests in such areas as Ojo Caliente, Española, and Arroyo Hondo, New Mexico, and Pueblo and San Luis, Colorado.

Because these projects took me to many of the village churches in northern New Mexico, I began to realize that although there were many photographic books of the major churches of New Mexico, there was no publication which showed the beauty of many of the smaller northern New Mexico churches. With this in mind, I contacted Jack Parsons, a photographer I had met when he produced a video documentary of my parents, nationally known tinsmiths Emilio and Senaida Romero, for which I did the narration. I asked Jack if he would compile photographs of these churches which could be incorporated into a book so that many people would be able to appreciate their beauty and distinctive architecture.

This book is not intended to be a scholarly treatise on the plethora of historical data available on these historic churches and their architecture. Rather, my hope is that it will be used as a guide to impart knowledge to everyone who is interested in northern New Mexico, local schoolchildren as well as tourists, and to encourage these people to discover for themselves the charm and enduring traditions of northern New Mexico's villages.

A short introduction to each area contains suggestions for tours or day trips, with the assumption that the traveler will be going in a circuitous route from south to north; these are only suggested routes among other possible trips the reader may plan.

In addition to the maps in this book, it is strongly recommended that travelers also use a current regional road map for each area. When touring the churches in remote villages, it may be necessary to consult a current road map to determine which roads are more easily traveled by four-wheel drive vehicles. Some areas may not be accessible during wet or snowy weather.

CHURCH AT CORDOVA, N.M., ca. 1935
Photo by T. Harmon Parkhurst. Courtesy Museum of New Mexico, Neg. No. 9031.

ACKNOWLEDGMENTS

I am indebted to the Archdiocese of Santa Fe, and particularly Marina Ochoa, Curator of the Patrimony for the Arts of the Archdiocese, for their support and permission to undertake this task, and for their neverending efforts to preserve the churches and missions which are the subject of this book. The Archdiocese has worked diligently toward this goal by establishing the Commission on Churches, which oversees all aspects of restoration and preservation.

In the early stages of research for this book, Victor Johnson allowed me to see the information contained in the architectural survey of churches done by his firm, Nestor & Johnson, which provided invaluable structural information.

I wish to thank Jack Parsons for his diligence in traversing many of the back roads and chasing the light to photograph these monuments to our ancestors' perseverance, as well as for his shared sense of humor in those instances when nobody showed up to open the churches for us.

Finally, thanks to Ann Mason, my editor, whose expertise was invaluable; I am especially grateful to Red Crane Books, which saw the possibilities in this publication and assisted me in making it a reality.

Marie Romero Cash

INTRODUCTION

Everywhere in Northern New Mexico there is extraordinary beauty: majestic mountains, historic villages, exceptional architecture, and diverse cultures. The picturesque adobe churches in this area are unique: they are monuments to the hardy priests and settlers who emigrated from Spain and New Spain to a remote frontier and who endured arduous travel, isolation, and the hardships of establishing themselves in colonial New Mexico in the seventeenth, eighteenth, and nineteenth centuries. Some of these churches are massive and elaborate, while others are small and plain, but each possesses a legacy which captivates the eye, the imagination, and the heart. Together they symbolize the profound dedication of the early priests and villagers, their love of family, and their deep faith in God.

Since colonists first arrived in northern New Mexico faith has been the cornerstone of the Hispanic family. Religious observances marked the cycle of the seasons as well as the passages of life. For these *vecinos*, original settlers, religious events became an important link to the cultural heritage of their distant homeland. They toiled with the priests not only to meet the daily needs of their lives, but also to provide places of worship; most of the village churches were built by members of the communities as a labor of reverence.

Several northern New Mexico churches date from the mid-1700s; others date from the early 1800s. After 1830, as the threat from Indian raids began to diminish, smaller communities were established in more remote areas, and many small chapels were built. Some of the larger twentieth-century churches have been built in pueblo or territorial style, in consonance with the surrounding architecture. The smaller mission churches were erected with whatever materials were available. Although puddled adobe had been used in buildings in New Mexico for centuries, the adobe brick made from varying proportions of mud, clay, and straw or manure was introduced by the Spaniards to the area as a building material. This mixture was formed into bricks using a simple wooden mold called an *adobero*, dried for several days on the ground, and then stacked. In colonial times adobe bricks measured 10 inches by 18 inches by 5 inches and weighed approximately 55 pounds, unlike modern adobes which measure 10 inches by 14 inches by 4 inches and weigh much less. In many instances the walls were then covered with adobe (mud) plaster made from three parts dirt, two parts sand, and one-half part flour to seal out wind and moisture.

The typical New Mexican church was built not only for religious services but also to be used as a fortress. It was surrounded by an *atrio*, a large walled yard in front which enclosed the church and *camposanto* (graveyard). Churches were generally built to give the impression of being two-story structures, although only the choir loft at the front of the church was on the second level. The high ceilings of the nave and sanctuary were supported by massive vigas, which rested on richly carved wooden corbels. In many instances the vigas were painted in bright reds and greens; traces of such decoration can still be seen in the 1830s church at El Rito. If the structure was not flanked by towers on each side, the parapet high above the main doorway generally contained one or two bells. Any auxiliary buildings needed to house the priests were added to the church as needed. There does not appear to be a totally standard style of construction for these churches; however, most of the larger churches seem to have been constructed in the cruciform (cross-shaped) style, although many churches, including the Santuario de Chimayó, were constructed in the single-nave style.

Until glass was imported later in the nineteenth century, windows utilizing sheets of selenite (mica) were set high on the walls and provided little light. Later, the transverse clerestory window was developed, providing effective lighting to the main altar area of the church. These windows, which provide light from one direction only, are only visible while looking up from the altar towards the back of the church. Additional interior lighting was provided by rows of candles on crossbars known as *aranas,* which were raised and lowered by ropes from the ceiling.

Franciscan priests were assigned to northern New Mexico pueblos by around 1600 in order to disseminate Christianity. Prior to 1800, visitations were made to New Mexico in 1730, 1737, and 1760 by bishops of Durango, Mexico, who were eager to assure the priests and colonists that they had complete authority over the churches in the province. Other visitations were made in 1808, 1818, and 1826. Each of the surveys done during these visitations provided historical data regarding the condition and furnishings of the churches, the lives of the Franciscan priests, and the population of the area. The most extensive of these ecclesiastical visitations was made in 1776 by Fray Francisco Atanasio Domínguez, a Franciscan priest who provided a complete account of what was occurring in colonial New Mexico. Domínguez recruited a mapmaker, Captain Bernardo Miera y Pacheco, to accompany him on his journey to what is now the state of Utah. Miera y Pacheco was also an artist whose religious artworks already graced several of the area churches. Since Domínguez came from Mexico City and was insensitive to the frontier, many of his opinions must be regarded from that perspective; for him, simple adobe churches were crude and unsophisticated in comparison with Mexican cathedrals.

In his inventories Domínguez described not only the distance between villages, but also the terrain and the ease or difficulty of travel between points. He also reported extensively on the customs of the villagers and on the area agriculture, including the types of fruit grown in each orchard. Moreover, he depicted the churches and their furnishings in great detail, even to the amount and type of lighting. Each piece of linen and silver was inventoried, as were the items of jewelry which adorned the statues. It is because of the richness of detail provided in these reports that we are today able to envision New Mexico colonial life as it existed.

The decoration of the church interiors became of utmost importance during the period when the major towns such as Santa Fe, Santa Cruz, and Las Trampas were established. Because of the great distance from their homeland, it was impossible for the priests and villagers to import all the necessary furnishings for the churches.

Consequently, they were increasingly supplied by local craftsmen. Although the villagers were from varied walks of life, many of them had built and furnished their own homes; and it was these *carpinteros* (carpenters) who provided the priests with wooden items needed for the churches, such as altar railings and church pews for the wealthy and their families. Rent was often paid for the church pews at the rate of one peso or more per year, and the money was used for the necessities of the church. Those parishioners who did not have prestige in the community, or who could not afford to rent the pews, had to stand during church services.

From the early artisans there emerged a group that came to be known as *santeros*, the painters and carvers of religious images, or *santos*. These santeros were artists, both trained and untrained, who painted images of the patron saints on pine panels and also carved and painted figures in the round. The art of the santero emerged because of the necessity to adorn churches and home altars. The hand-adzed panels of pine which they coated with a mixture of cooked gypsum and animal glue and then painted with pigments made from plant and mineral sources are known as *retablos*; and the images carved in the round, gessoed and painted in much the same manner are known as *bultos*. As buildings were completed, large altar screens were constructed of pine panels surrounded by carved pillars. These large multipaneled altar screens, constructed of wooden beams with hand-adzed pine panels inserted between them, and gessoed and painted with images of saints, are known either as *reredos* or retablos. In many instances oil paintings which had been donated to the church by the king of Spain were incorporated into the altar screens rather than painted pine panels. The eighteenth-century carved stone altar of the military chapel (La Castrense) which stood on the south side of the plaza in Santa Fe until 1850 was used as a model for nearly all the large altar screens painted during this time.

Some of the earliest santero art in New Mexican churches was done at Laguna and Ácoma pueblo churches, although the artwork at both churches has been heavily overpainted in recent years. In the northern part of the state, remaining examples of santero work can still be seen at the churches in Chimayó, Truchas, Las Trampas, and Ranchos de Taos, and in Santa Fe at San Miguel Church, where guided tours are conducted daily. Many of the smaller churches contain examples of this folk art, but few of these churches are open to the public on an ongoing basis; and in many instances the santos have been taken home by the caretakers rather than left in empty, unprotected churches.

Although numerous santeros created images for the various churches beginning in the last quarter of the eighteenth century, most of the santos which remain in the churches today were executed by two santeros, José Rafael Aragón (referred to as Rafael Aragón) and Molleno. Rafael Aragón, whose career spanned some forty-two years beginning in approximately 1820, was by far the most popular and prolific of the santeros, his work gracing many of the major churches. Today, many of his works are housed in museums and private collections, although a significant number of them still remain in the churches for which they were originally made. Rafael Aragón was an extremely versatile artist, being proficient both in painting panels and carving images, and it is speculated he may have established a *taller*, or workshop, to meet the great demand for his work. In addition to building and painting massive altar screens for churches at such locations as Chimayó and Santa Cruz, he was also skilled at carving smaller santos. He portrayed the popular saints of the era strongly and sensitively, with careful attention paid to detail. In general, his works are considered to be more original and expressive than the works of later santeros, who relied much more on traditional religious sources.

Many New Mexican santeros remain anonymous to this day, since they tended to subordinate their own identities to the greater importance of their sacred art. Others, such as the Laguna Santero, are only named for the location where they created major works. Although the Laguna Santero is best known for his work at the Laguna Pueblo church, considerable new evidence has surfaced in the past several years to link this santero to several churches in the northern area. The names of only a few santeros are known, such as Molleno, Pedro Antonio Fresquís, José Rafael Aragón, and José Aragón (no relation to José Rafael Aragón). José Aragón, who worked for only a short time in the mountain villages of northern

New Mexico, produced a large body of work from 1820–1835, dating and signing several of his panels. His only known major large works remaining are the two altar screens he built and painted for the Santuario de Chimayó, both containing exquisite paintings still in their original condition. A number of altar screens by Molleno, whose work spanned a period of thirty years from 1800–1830, still remain intact in several of the churches. His main altar screen at the Santuario de Chimayó is a dazzling assemblage of painted scrolls, flowers, and geometric designs which frame the large, carved wooden crucifix, Our Lord of Esquípulas (Nuestro Señor de Esquípulas), an image of Christ crucified on the tree of life. The niche itself is surrounded by a gesso-relief design covered with gold leaf. Molleno also painted one of the side altar screens in a style different from that of the main screen—apparently at a later date. In addition, he painted altar screens at Ranchos de Taos and at Talpa. His personal style is highly original and does not appear to have been influenced by earlier santeros; nor does it appear to have significantly influenced later santeros. Although the work of several other santeros still exists in some of the northern New Mexico churches, these santeros are not as well known as those already mentioned, and they did not produce major bodies of work.

In general, the santeros created an indigenous folk art that is distinctive and unique—one that cannot be compared to other art forms without taking into consideration the need which generated it. For over 200 years it has been described in many (often derogatory) terms—as primitive, barbaric, or ugly. Nevertheless, santero art has a strength and beauty all its own and has survived its many critics.

Over the years, many of the eighteenth- and nineteenth-century churches of northern New Mexico were partially or totally destroyed by those who attempted to modernize them. A great number of the buildings collapsed when, in an effort to facilitate water drainage due to rain and snow, pitched roofs were constructed to replace the original flat roofs. Usually it was not the weight of the new roof which caused it to collapse, but rather the fact that bond beams were not used or that pitched roofs were added without walls being tied.

In addition, many churches were completely transformed after Jean Baptiste Lamy, a French priest, arrived in Santa Fe in 1851 to undertake his duties as bishop. He was appalled at what he perceived as the crudeness and lack of sophistication of the regional adobe churches. By 1875, when he was appointed archbishop, the modernization process of the existing churches was in full swing in Santa Fe and the surrounding areas. Pitched roofs, belfries, and spires were added to the structures. Many of the furnishings, including the altar screens and santos, were burned or discarded, and replaced with "wedding cake" tiered marble altars and plaster of paris statues. There were, however, many parishioners in the northern villages who refused to part with the images which had adorned their mission churches long before the French priests arrived. These villagers protected and cared for their santos, removing them from the churches to their homes, and continued to worship in the style to which they were accustomed. As a result of these early preservation efforts, many of the northern churches still contain examples of the captivating folk art which Lamy found so barbaric.

Many of the customs and religious festivals established in colonial times are still observed and celebrated today. The annual celebration of the saints' feast days were, and still are, solemn occasions. The music of guitars and tambourines mingled in the air, and guns were fired. Each year the patron saint of the village chapel was honored with a fiesta, a *funcion*, which usually continued into the late hours of the night. Preparation for the fiesta always consisted of cooking the traditional foods: beans, chile, posole, and tortillas, along with the usual *chicharones* (fried pork rinds) and meat pies, followed by desserts of every kind, *empanaditas*, *bizcochitos*, and *buñuelos*. Vespers were held the evening before, and the morning of the fiesta Holy Mass was celebrated, after which the patron saint was placed on an *anda*, a wooden carrier, and transported by four parishioners at the head of a procession, followed by the priest and the villagers. A guitarist usually strummed as the villagers sang hymns. Then the santo was returned to the church, and the other festivities began.

In many villages the feast of Saint Isidore the Farmer (San

Isidro Labrador) on May 15 has been celebrated by a procession of the villagers, all farmers, who would carry the patron saint to the farm farthest from the church. The statue was then placed in a willow niche, and candles were lit around it. Bonfires were built, and the villagers gathered around and sang hymns and prayed the rosary. Food was served at midnight, after which everyone slept. Early the next morning, the carved image of Saint Isidore was carried to all the farm fields in the village so that the crops would be blessed, thereby assuring a good harvest in the autumn. As the procession neared the church, the church bells would begin to ring, and the image of Saint Isidore would be placed next to the altar.

At fiesta time in the larger villages, events such as rodeos, religious dramas, and beauty pageants were often held; but regardless of the size of the village, there was always a dance. The entire village, as well as people from the surrounding areas, would attend, whether Catholic or not, because the festivities were not only colorful, but provided a respite from the hard work of daily survival. The *corrida del gallo*, or rooster pull, was often a favorite event in the festivities. It was a contest in which opposing groups of horsemen took turns lassoing a rooster that had been buried in the ground up to its neck. The winner was the group which had the rooster in its possession by the time the game was over. This event was usually held in the villages on the feast day of Saint John (San Juan), June 24.

Each year on or before Christmas Day at several of the Indian pueblos and northern villages a Matachines Dance is held and continues daily through New Year's Day. The origins of this dance can be traced back to the seventeenth century, and it is believed the dance was taught to the Indians by Franciscan priests. The dance troupes are comprised of men wearing black pants and vests. Varicolored scarves cover their mouths, and their eyes are hidden by a black fringe. On their heads are bishops' miters from which radiate brightly colored silk streamers. The only female participant is a young girl called La Malinche, who, dressed in a communion-like white dress and sweater, represents Good. She dances alone or with the male soloist, El Monarca (said to represent Montezuma), whose identifying feature is the cross which tops his funnel-shaped crown. The role of *el toro* (the bull), representing Evil, is generally played by a young man wearing a papier-mâché bull's head and dancing with two sticks that represent his front legs. The *abuelos*, or grandfather figures, wear masks and carry whips in an attempt to terrorize the audience. This pageantry is accompanied by the music of violins, drums, and guitars.

During these feast day celebrations, it is generally the custom to install the new *mayordomos*, the caretakers which will serve the church for the coming year. Although the responsibilities assigned to these mayordomos vary with each church or mission, traditionally their duties include keeping the church and the surrounding areas clean and functioning, and making sure all details regarding the operation of the church are taken care of. The mayordomo system was developed shortly after the resettlement of New Mexico in the late seventeenth century, following the Pueblo Revolt of 1680. The scarcity of priests in the remote village areas made the upkeep of the increasing number of churches difficult, and the mayordomo system was developed whereby various parishioners were appointed to take care of the many details that the priest could not attend to. This system has endured over the years, and almost every church and mission today still has mayordomos. They are the keepers of the keys and make sure the church is open or closed at specific times, that the floors are swept and clean, the linens are changed, and that the priest is notified of anything that needs to be called to his attention. In addition, they take care of electrical and plumbing matters as well as arrange for other repairs to the interior and exterior of the church. In sparsely populated missions, the same mayordomos serve for periods sometimes exceeding ten years. Their help is invaluable to the priests and parishioners, who depend on them to facilitate the continued functioning of the churches.

Another custom observed well into the twentieth century was the practice, during funeral processions, of placing a wooden cross wherever the casket of the deceased was placed on the ground. The participants in the procession would then rest, pray, and meditate. These crosses, known as *descansos*, can still be seen on the way to the cemetery in most villages. A similar type of cross is still placed by residents of rural communities along the roadside where a fatal accident has occurred. Today, northern New Mexico is known for such crosses incorporated into the landscape and for its colorful historic graveyards that surround many of the village churches.

Considering the rapid population growth and modernization which have occurred in New Mexico in recent years, it is gratifying that many villages have retained their old customs to this day. Villagers continue to worship in the same manner, and their profound religious beliefs and love of the earth are intact; the churches are still maintained on an ongoing basis, and the feast days are celebrated in much the same way. In these villages of the rural north, the trappings of modernity have not made as noticeable an impact as they have in the more populous urban areas of New Mexico.

Each of the churches in northern New Mexico has a unique character and history of its own which is well worth exploring; as a whole they represent a significant contribution to New Mexico's cultural heritage. There is an undying need among the villagers to retain bountiful memories of the past within the walls of each and every one of these long-established monuments to their God; in fact, so important are these edifices to the villagers that in recent years they have undertaken many restoration projects involving the churches which are in need of repair. The recent joint efforts of parishioners and restoration organizations, such as the New Mexico Community Foundation, to stabilize, rebuild, and replaster community churches of the north is a testimony to the significance of these churches to the cultural identity of the region.

VISITORS' ETIQUETTE

For various reasons many of the churches, particularly the smaller missions, are not open to the public except for masses, funerals, and feast days; although feast days are not always observed in every church, many are still celebrated in the traditional manner. Pueblo churches are rarely open to the public. However, these churches can be fully appreciated from the outside, as the exterior architecture of each has a distinctive beauty.

In the event admission is gained to any of these churches, careful attention must be given to demeanor and attire. As in any place of worship, no matter what its location, the exercise of common sense is of paramount importance. It is advisable not to wear clothes which overexpose the body or to speak loudly. Children should be supervised and not allowed to run or scream in churches, and pets should be left outside. Many times there are parishioners present who are immersed in meditation and prayer. The use of flash with cameras, particularly if a funeral mass is in progress, is not recommended. Out of respect for the family, it is best to leave the church and return after the funeral is over.

Religious images in the churches should never be touched; many of them are over 200 years old and irreplaceable. Because of the possibility of fires, votive candles should not be lit in those churches which are not open on an ongoing basis. All cigarettes should be extinguished before entering the church; drinks and food should be left outside; and any trash should be disposed of properly.

Each Indian pueblo has specific regulations regarding photography of its church and dances. These dances are not only social events, but religious ceremonies to be observed with respect. It is essential for photographers to inquire about photographic policies before attending dances at the various pueblos, as cameras may be confiscated if used without permission. In addition, the Archdiocese of Santa Fe has a policy which prohibits the photography of churches for any purpose other than personal use without permission and payment of a fee. Professional photographers are encouraged to contact the Archdiocese of Santa Fe, Office of Historic Patrimony and Archives, 321 Cathedral Place, Santa Fe, New Mexico 87501, (505) 983-3811, to obtain the necessary forms and fee requirements. These regulations may be posted at some of the larger churches.

The churches of northern New Mexico have all survived for many years, some for several centuries, because of the diligence of parishioners, who have maintained them in as pristine a condition as possible. Visitors should respect this heritage and the privilege of being allowed to view these historic sites.

CHURCH AT SANTA CRUZ, N.M., ca. 1935
Photo by T. Harmon Parkhurst. Courtesy Museum of New Mexico, Neg. No. 9808.

CHAPTER ONE

The Santa Fe Area

SANTA FE *makes an excellent base for touring the churches of northern New Mexico. Founded in 1610, it is the oldest capital in the United States. During Spanish rule, 1598–1821, it was the capital of an isolated province, but with Mexican independence in 1821, trade opened up and the historic Santa Fe Trail was established. In 1846, the Territory of New Mexico became part of the United States. The varied landscape of the high desert and mountains, the blending of Indian, Hispanic, and Anglo-American cultures, the prevalence of territorial-style architecture, and the presence of numerous artists and diverse galleries all combine to make Santa Fe the "city different." In spite of considerable growth, the city has retained its architectural integrity; a large number of homes and buildings are on the National Historic Register. Some of the most interesting of these historic buildings are the churches.*

Before embarking on a tour of the churches around Santa Fe, it is wise to determine whether it will be accomplished by walking or by driving. Although Santa Fe has some long city blocks, several of the churches discussed here are within a short distance of the plaza area. It is possible to walk from the plaza to Saint Francis Cathedral, the Loretto Chapel, and San Miguel Church in the same day. At another time the Santuario de Guadalupe can be reached easily on foot from the plaza. The remaining churches are best visited by car because of the distances which separate them. Special consideration must be given when desiring to visit Rosario Chapel. It is rarely open to the public, and parking is not readily available if a funeral is in progress. However, there is usually a caretaker on the grounds who can direct visitors to the chapel.

S A N   I S I D R O

Agua Fria Village

*L*OCATED ON AGUA FRIA STREET IN AGUA FRIA Village, just outside the Santa Fe city limits, this adobe church was built in 1835. It has an asphalt-shingled pitched roof and a belfry, which was added later. The interior has a ceiling composed of 10-inch vigas and corbels, a concrete floor, and large wall niches. The church artwork consists of a contemporary altar screen painted by Santa Fe santero Luis Tapia, and tin-framed stations of the cross adorn the walls.

At the turn of the century, there were two sugarcane mills located near the church. Many of the older residents recall with delight that they used to watch the villagers bring their cane to the presses for crushing, and that they would wait in anticipation for the first taste of syrup after it had been boiled from the cane. After Sunday mass the children would ride on the crossbeam of the press as it revolved in the cane-crushing process, and the adults would dance on the patio.

Productions of *Los Pastores*, a well-known Christmas play, were staged by villagers for many years as part of the Christmas festivities.

SAN ISIDRO
Agua Fria Village
FEAST DAY: May 15

SANTUARIO DE GUADALUPE

Santa Fe

*B*UILT AS A SHRINE TO HONOR THE MEXICAN VIR-
gin, Our Lady of Guadalupe (Nuestra Señora de Guadalupe), this
church is believed to be the first Guadalupe shrine in the United
States. In the center of the historic Guadalupe District of Santa
Fe, the church is located 1/2 mile southwest of the plaza at the
corner of Guadalupe and Agua Fria streets, on the east bank of
the Santa Fe River. With its uncluttered lines and beautiful grounds,
it is one of the most attractive churches in New Mexico.

Although the license for construction was issued in 1795, the
building date for this church has not been precisely pinpointed;
however, it is estimated to be sometime after the date of the issuance
of the license. The building is a massive adobe structure, in the
cruciform (cross-shaped) plan, a style used primarily in the larger,
more important churches. It originally had a large tower with copper
bells said to have been made locally. The choir loft has handsome
carved vigas and corbels.

The main altar houses an oil painting on canvas of an altar
screen dated 1783 in the left-hand corner and signed by the Mexican
artist José de Alcibar, and it is likely that this was painted before
the church was dedicated. After 1880, the church was remodeled:
the dirt floor was covered with wood flooring, windows were cut
into the massive walls, and a pitched shingle roof was added. The
adobe exterior has periodically been mud-plastered over the last
century.

Sometime after 1920, the church became an independent
mission. Because of the increase in the number of parishioners,
a massive new church was completed nearby in December 1961,
leaving the old church virtually inactive until 1975. At that time
it was deeded by the Archdiocese of Santa Fe to the Guadalupe

SANTUARIO DE GUADALUPE
Santa Fe
FEAST DAY: December 12

Historic Foundation, which assumed responsibility for maintaining the facility and still continues in that function under a 1991 lease agreement with the Archdiocese. The foundation has undertaken several restoration projects on the building, although these projects are not looked upon favorably by most historic preservationists. During remodeling in 1989, many graves were discovered as workers dug a foundation at the front entrance to the church. The remains were reinterred in the same place they were discovered, accompanied by a religious service. Remodeling and restoration have been continued through 1991, and after much controversy about the effects of hard-plaster, a combination of mud and lime plaster was applied to the structure.

Because of the reverence held by many for Our Lady of Guadalupe, religious services are still held at the Santuario on the 12th day of each month at 12:12 P.M.; in addition, the Guadalupe Historic Foundation has sponsored many well-attended cultural events over the years.

S A N M I G U E L

Santa Fe

$\mathcal{T}$HIS MASSIVE CHURCH IS LOCATED A FEW BLOCKS from the plaza at the corner of De Vargas Street and the Old Santa Fe Trail. There is ongoing disagreement about the actual construction date of San Miguel Church. It is considered by some historians to be the oldest place of religious worship still in use in North America. According to various published reports, the original church was built sometime after 1605 and destroyed by fire during the Pueblo Revolt of 1680. It is situated on the south side of the Santa Fe River in a historic area referred to as "Barrio de Analco," meaning "neighborhood on the other side of the water."

Construction was begun on a new church in 1693 and completed in 1710. An inscription on one of the vigas reads: *"El Señor Marques de la Penuela hizo esta fábrica, el Alferes Real Don Augustín Flores Vergara, su criado. Año de 1710."* ("His lordship, the Marquis de la Penuela, erected this building assisted by the Royal Ensign Don Augustín Flores Vergara, his servant. The year 1710.")

More than a century later, in 1830, the roof was replaced and paid for by a prominent Santa Fe citizen, Don Simon Delgado, whose descendants still reside in Santa Fe. During this renovation, only two of the original vigas were left on the structure. In 1872, during a heavy rainstorm, the upper tower collapsed, and the building remained in a state of disrepair until 1887, when it was restored and stone buttresses were added to strengthen it.

San Miguel has a trapezoidal apse, a flat roof, and a ceiling comprised of vigas, corbels, decorative moldings, and trim.

The mission bell, now displayed inside, weighs 780 pounds. The date on the side indicates it was cast in 1356, but noted historian E. Boyd conjectured that the date was actually 1856. The bell bears

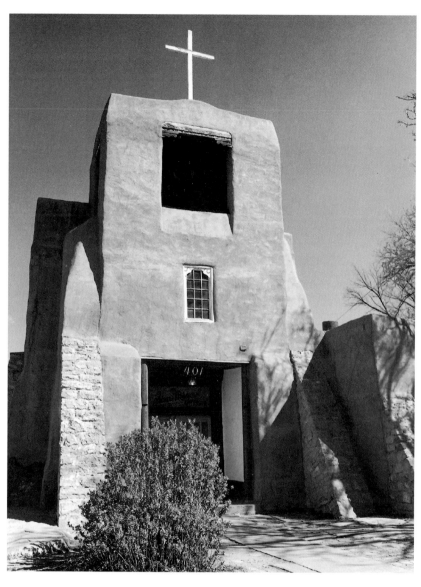

SAN MIGUEL
Santa Fe

FEAST DAY: September 29

the inscription, *"San José, ruega por nosotros"* ("Saint Joseph, pray for us").

Most of the artwork in the church is part of the original seventeenth- and eighteenth-century decor, and therefore includes fine early examples of santero art. The altar screen was painted in 1798 for the church by the Laguna Santero, so named because of his work at the Laguna Pueblo church. The oil paintings which hang on the walls on each side of the altar date to the late 1600s and reputedly occupied the original building. There are several paintings on tanned buffalo hides which date to the mid-eighteenth century, along with several other examples of nineteenth-century santero carvings on niches and pedestals at the altar. The representation of the patron saint of the church, Saint Michael (San Miguel), is an eighteenth-century gessoed and polychromed Mexican carving, but the tinwork on the altar is contemporary. Audio tours of the church are conducted regularly, and the gift shop provides a booklet about the intriguing history of the church and the artwork contained in it.

L O R E T T O   C H A P E L

Santa Fe

*L*OCATED AT 219 OLD SANTA FE TRAIL, SEVERAL blocks from the plaza near the Inn at Loretto, this chapel has a colorful history fraught with mystery.

Almost 150 years ago the Sisters of Loretto left Kentucky to travel to Santa Fe, then a small town populated primarily by Spanish, Mexican, and Indian people. After a long, arduous journey, they arrived in Santa Fe and established a convent under the guidance of Bishop Lamy. The Academy of Our Lady of Light was opened in 1853, several years after their arrival, and by 1890 had an enrollment of fifty boarders; the convent was not established until some twenty years later.

At Lamy's request, the Loretto Chapel was designed after the Sainte-Chapelle in Paris by architect Projectus Mouly and was dedicated on April 25, 1878. It was described in the local paper in 1875 as being constructed of cut stone from a quarry east of the city. The hand-blown stained-glass windows were made to order in France. The superb massive doorway, still used today, is 18 feet high, while the chapel itself measures 25 feet wide, 75 feet long, and 85 feet high. The structure, built in Gothic style with a choir loft at the rear, heralded the arrival of education to the area, since in 1853 the Sisters of Loretto had opened the Academy of Our Lady of Light at Santa Fe, and the chapel bore the name of Our Lady of Light. By 1869, the sisters had established schools all over New Mexico, and the massive chapel remained a tribute to their dedication.

It was not until the chapel was nearly completed that a disturbing discovery was made: there was no stairway connecting its two levels. Many carpenters were consulted to correct the problem, but they

LORETTO CHAPEL

Santa Fe

FEAST DAY: none

were unable to come up with an adequate solution, and the project was abandoned.

As the legend goes, the sisters then began a novena to Saint Joseph, to whom they were quite close, and on the last day of the novena a gray-haired man with a donkey appeared at the convent and offered to assist the sisters in the building of a stairway. It is unclear just how long the work took—estimates range from two weeks to eight months; however, the old man constructed entirely from wood a 23-foot-high spiral staircase that made two complete 360-degree turns and had 33 steps, using only a saw, T-square, hammer, and wooden pegs to secure it. Then he disappeared as mysteriously as he had come.

This spiral stairway at the front of the chapel leading to the choir loft has no center support; it rests against the loft at the top and on the floor at the bottom. The railing was added two years after its completion. Moreover, the fact that the stairway was built completely with wooden pegs, rather than nails, makes its design even more intriguing. Architects and builders from many areas have come to view and inspect the staircase, expressing the opinion that, according to its construction, it should have collapsed when first used. Although various claims have been made over the past century regarding the identity of the carpenter who built the stairway, the family of a master Austrian carpenter has been the most diligent and persuasive in its claim that it was their ancestor, a man named Hadwiger, who constructed it. And even though the stairway may have actually been built by any one of the proposed men, the local legend persists, after the stairway has been used continuously for over 100 years, that the carpenter who built it was actually Saint Joseph (San José).

The Academy of Our Lady of Light closed in 1968, and by 1970 the chapel was being managed by the Historic Santa Fe Foundation. In 1971, the Kirkpatrick family, owners of the adjoining hotel, the Inn at Loretto, acquired all rights to the chapel and continues to maintain it to this day.

SAINT FRANCIS CATHEDRAL

Santa Fe

*F*OR CENTURIES A STRIKING MONUMENT NEAR THE plaza in downtown Santa Fe, this massive church has a long and colorful history. Originally built as a *parroquia* (parish church) in 1714, it survived for a century and a half as the parish for the area. Although there were remodeling efforts prior to 1806, the most extensive renovation of the structure began after Jean Baptiste Lamy (made famous in Willa Cather's novel *Death Comes for the Archbishop*) was named bishop of Santa Fe in 1851. According to historical accounts, the conversion of Romanesque style was viewed by Lamy as a necessary modernization which would relieve Santa Fe of its crude pueblo look and give it badly needed sophistication. The reconstruction began in 1860, an arduous undertaking which would ordinarily have left the parishioners without a church for several years; however, in order to avoid this inconvenience, it was decided that the new brick edifice could be built around the existing church. Even though Lamy brought European architects and stonemasons from his homeland, progress was slow. In 1875, he was appointed New Mexico's first archbishop, and some years later traveled to France to raise funds for the construction, which had virtually come to a halt and would not recommence until 1880.

In 1884, by the time removal of the interior adobe building was to begin, Lamy again began fund-raising efforts, At the time of his retirement in 1885, only the nave of the cathedral had been completed. Subsequently, his bishop coadjutor, J. B. Salpointe, was appointed archbishop and undertook the task of completing the massive edifice after Lamy's death on February 14, 1888. Construction continued for several more years until finally, on October 18, 1895, some twenty-six years after renovations had begun, the church was ready for rededication. Although the new church was not completely as Lamy had envisioned it, and sections of the old parroquia still remained, the transformation from an old adobe building to a massive French-style church was achieved: the roof is pitched, metal on wood frame; the nave is Romanesque-Byzantine style with vaulted ceilings, and there are stone columns with Corinthian capitals supporting the arches and cross vaults; the terrazzo floors gleam in the sunlight.

In 1957, a stone coffin with the remains of two priests was reinterred in the west wall niche. The coffin had been removed from the old parroquia sanctuary wall, where it had been for more than two centuries. Archbishop Lamy is buried in the crypt behind the altar.

The chapel at the rear left of the church, dedicated to Our Lady of the Conquest (La Conquistadora), is constructed of adobe with a painted plaster interior. It has a pitched copper roof, and the ceiling is composed of vigas with split *latillas* between and edged by carved corbels. The chapel contains an altar constructed and painted in the tradition of the eighteenth and nineteenth centuries; the original church apparently did not contain any of the santero work found so offensive by Lamy.

The elaborately dressed statue of La Conquistadora, which was brought from New Spain (Mexico) with the original settlers in the early 1600s, is featured prominently during the Santa Fe Fiesta, held each year since 1712 on a weekend in mid-September to commemorate the peaceful reconquest of Santa Fe by Don Diego de Vargas in 1692. The area had been occupied by Indians since the 1680 Pueblo Revolt. Fiesta begins on Friday with a proclamation and mass held at Rosario Chapel and continues with the burning of a large effigy called Zozobra (Old Man Gloom) that evening at dusk, an event attended annually by tens of thousands of people. The festivities end Sunday evening with a candlelight procession to the Cross of the Martyrs on a hill above Santa Fe. During Fiesta a queen is chosen, as well as a man who portrays Don Diego de Vargas, the conqueror who carried the statue of La Conquistadora back to Santa Fe from Mexico, where it had been taken during the 1680 Pueblo Revolt.

In the last few years a large contemporary altar screen has

been installed at the main altar of Saint Francis Cathedral, painted by Albuquerque artist Robert Lentz, whose style is reminiscent of Greek icons. The screen is comprised of fifteen panels of saints surrounded by ornately carved pillars.

In 1920, the Franciscan friars took charge of the Saint Francis Cathedral, and have continued to maintain it to the present time. The great spruce trees and the *sabina macha* (creeping juniper) surrounding the La Conquistadora Chapel were brought from the Jemez Mountains and planted in the 1930s by Santa Fe tinsmith Emilio R. Romero, the author's father, who was then employed by the United States Forest Service. These trees still tower over the chapel today.

SAINT FRANCIS CATHEDRAL
Santa Fe
FEAST DAY: October 4

C R I S T O   R E Y

Santa Fe

CRISTO REY CHURCH WAS BUILT IN 1939 ON UPPER Canyon Road to commemorate the 400th anniversary of Francisco Vásquez de Coronado's expedition to the Southwest. In addition, it was to serve as a majestic setting for the great carved stone altar screen from the 1760s military chapel of Our Lady of Light, which had been stored for many years in the side chapel of Saint Francis Cathedral.

The church, reputed to be the largest adobe church in America, was designed by famed architect John Gaw Meem and is considered a great monument of the Spanish-pueblo revival. It is 125 feet long, 40 feet wide, and 33 feet high, and is built from over 150,000 adobes, which were made by the parishioners; the walls range in thickness from 2 to 9 feet. The vigas, corbels, and latillas were brought from nearby New Mexico forests; the doors, pews, confessionals, and iron light fixtures were made by students at the Diocesan Lourdes Trade School in Albuquerque.

Inside is one of the most famous pieces of church art in New Mexico. This great stone altar screen, or reredos, is composed of three pieces of carved white stone, decorated with representations of God, various saints, angels, and flowers. The stone was quarried northwest of Santa Fe and carved in 1760 by unknown artisans brought to New Mexico by Governor Francisco Antonio Marín del Valle for the military chapel being erected on the Santa Fe Plaza. It is carved on three levels with a lunette top-piece above the screen. The upper lunette contains an image of God the Father; the first (top) level contains an image of Our Lady of Valvanera (Nuestra Señora de Valvanera); the second (middle) level contains images of Saint Joseph (San José), Saint James (Santiago), and Saint John Nepomuck (San Juan Nepomuceno); and the third (bottom) level

CRISTO REY
Santa Fe
FEAST DAY: last Sunday in November

contains images of Saint Ignatius of Loyola (San Ignacio de Loyola), Our Lady of Light (Nuestra Señora de la Luz), and Saint Francis Solano (San Francisco Solano). The panel of Our Lady of Light is a stone plaque given by Archbishop Lamy to the new Academy of Our Lady of Light in 1859; at some point it became incorporated into the altar screen. This magnificent altar screen is illuminated by a clerestory window, through which the morning sun shines.

R O S A R I O   C H A P E L

Santa Fe

*T*HE ORIGINAL CHAPEL ON THIS SITE AT THE corner of Paseo de Peralta and Guadalupe streets, 1/2 mile from the plaza, was erected in 1693 and dedicated to the statue of Our Lady of the Rosary (renamed La Conquistadora), which resides most of the year in Saint Francis Cathedral. This famous statue was taken by retreating Spanish settlers to El Paso del Norte (present-day El Paso, Texas) during the 1680 Pueblo Revolt and returned by De Vargas in 1693 during the reconquest of Santa Fe. A new chapel was paid for and built by Antonio José Ortiz in 1807; it is located on the site of the old chapel where De Vargas and his army are said to have camped in 1692 and is surrounded by a cemetery which has been in continuous use since the late 1700s. Although it is said that after his death in 1860 Ortiz was buried beneath the original chapel as a tribute to his generosity, in his last will and testament he requested that he be buried in the oratory at his home (presently the site of the Hilton Hotel) near the Santa Fe Plaza.

Rosario Chapel is of adobe construction with a pitched metal roof. The facade has been referred to as California mission style, and there are buttresses on the east side. The interior has wood floors and walls of painted plaster; the original vigas and corbels still exist in the old section of the building. The chapel was renovated in 1914 to accommodate the large crowds present each year during the services honoring La Conquistadora.

The heavily overpainted nineteenth-century altar screen in the chapel has been attributed to the santero Pedro Antonio Fresquís (working dates 1780–1831) by Alan Vedder, former Curator of Spanish Colonial Art at the Museum of New Mexico, although not enough of the original remains to verify this. This old altar screen is flanked by a contemporary altar screen carved and painted by artist Eugenie

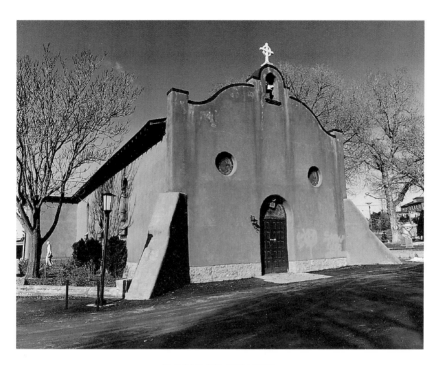

ROSARIO CHAPEL
Santa Fe
FEAST DAY: October 7

Shonnard, and a replica statue of La Conquistadora carved by
Gustave Baumann, which is kept at Rosario Chapel throughout the
year except during the novena. In addition, a recent mural by Santa
Fe artist Federico Vigil decorates the nave wall.

De Vargas's vow of eternal remembrance to the Virgin for her
assistance in the peaceful reconquest of Santa Fe has been celebrated
annually since the 1800s with a procession from the Saint Francis
Cathedral, where La Conquistadora is enthroned, to Rosario Chapel,
where she remains for one week. This novena is held each year
the week of June 4 through June 11.

SAN DIEGO DE TESUQUE

Tesuque Pueblo

*T*HIS CHURCH IS NESTLED IN THE CENTER OF centuries-old Tesuque Pueblo, a Tewa-speaking Indian settlement on U.S. 285, 6 miles north of Santa Fe. The Tewa name of the village translates to "cottonwood tree place." The original church, built before 1630, was called San Lorenzo de Tesuque. It was destroyed during the Pueblo Revolt of 1680, and the priest Fray Juan Bautista Pío became the first martyr of that uprising. When the church was rebuilt in 1695, it was renamed San Diego de Tesuque. It was rebuilt again in both 1740 and 1877, and has undergone additional renovation since 1970 when the Franciscan fathers of the Cathedral Parish in Santa Fe assumed its caretaking.

San Diego de Tesuque is of pueblo-style adobe construction with a flat roof and stuccoed walls. The parapet above the main doorway contains an old bell, and the interior has wood floors, vigas, and corbels. Although historians indicate that this church originally contained a santero altar screen, it is not known when or why it was removed. Perhaps it was destroyed before the church was rebuilt in 1877.

The feast day celebration centers around various traditional Indian dances. The Matachines Dance is held on Christmas Day, and in late May or early June the Corn Dance is held at the pueblo.

SAN DIEGO DE TESUQUE
Tesuque Pueblo
FEAST DAY: November 12

NUESTRA SEÑORA DE GUADALUPE

Cañada de los Alamos

CAÑADA DE LOS ALAMOS, MEANING "RAVINE OF the cottonwoods," is located off County Road 61, near Old Pecos Trail, about 15 miles past the Museum of International Folk Art. The village was established by a grant given to Lorenzo Marques on October 7, 1785, who was placed in possession by Antonio José Ortiz, senior administrative official and war captain, under authority of the Spanish Crown. The adobe church was not built until 1922, apparently since villagers preferred to attend services at nearby Cañoncito. It has a corrugated metal pitched roof with a louvered wooden belfry and double-hung windows. The interior has wood floors and a barrel-vaulted wood frame ceiling.

NUESTRA SEÑORA DE GUADALUPE

Cañada de los Alamos

FEAST DAY: December 12

CHAPTER TWO

The Española Area

THE ESPAÑOLA VALLEY *is the heart of the northern Indian pueblo country as well as the cradle of Spanish civilization in New Mexico. Its rich and colorful history is often overlooked because of emphasis placed on the "lowrider" phenomenon: automobiles which have been lowered and customized and which travel the roads around Española at a leisurely pace. Don Juan de Oñate, New Mexico's first colonizer, focused his efforts on this area during the late 1500s, establishing the first political capital of New Mexico in 1598 at San Juan Pueblo, near the confluence of the Río Grande and the Chama River. He called the new town San Juan de los Caballeros in honor of his own saint's day and the Spanish* caballeros *(horsemen) like himself who had come to colonize New Mexico. Soon, Oñate moved the settlement to the west side of the Río Grande and renamed it San Gabriel del Yunque; this site, now marked by a simple cross, is 5 miles north of Española, across the river from San Juan Pueblo.*

To tour the historic churches of the area, drive north from Santa Fe on U.S. 84/285 to a junction at the town of Pojoaque; the left fork, N.M. 502 in the direction of Los Alamos to N.M. 30, will provide a circuitous route around Española back to the road returning to Santa Fe. By following this route, several Indian pueblo churches and a number of village churches may be visited. The parish churches at Española, San Juan Pueblo, and Santa Cruz may be open during the day, but the smaller mission churches can only be viewed from the outside. In this area there are a number of mission churches scattered along colorful back roads, which provide a welcome respite from driving the main highway.

SAN ANTONIO DE PADUA

El Rancho

*L*OCATED JUST WEST OF EL RANCHO NEAR SAN Ildefonso Pueblo on N.M. 502, this adobe church was built in 1938 on the site of the previous church. At the time the church was being built, the villagers were still performing a folk drama called *Los Comanches*, which commemorated a skirmish between Spanish soldiers and Comanche warriors, staged on the day before the feast day of Saint Anthony of Padua (San Antonio de Padua). During mass, which was held with open doors, the jingling of sleigh bells could be heard by the parishioners, indicating that the actors, dressed as Comanche Indians, were busy pilfering items from automobiles, wagons, and buggies parked near the church. They also captured bystanders not attending church and held them for ransom. The villagers then had to redeem their belongings by paying the players for them.

After mass, a procession formed at the church door, headed by a wooden image of the patron saint, Saint Anthony of Padua, which had been placed on a carrier decorated with flowers. The procession also included colorfully dressed Indians wearing plumed headdresses and sleigh bells, people on horseback representing the Spaniards, and members of the Penitente Brotherhood singing *alabados* (hymns). After the procession circled the church, the image of Saint Anthony was carried inside, and the crowd converged at the banks of the arroyo to witness the reenactment of the battle between the Spaniards and Cuerno Verde, an Apache chief.

SAN ANTONIO DE PADUA

El Rancho

FEAST DAY: June 16

SAN ILDEFONSO

San Ildefonso Pueblo

*S*AN ILDEFONSO IS A TEWA-SPEAKING PUEBLO 10 miles south of Española on N.M. 502, about 28 miles from Santa Fe. It is situated in the middle of a wide plain hemmed in by mountains, in close proximity to Santa Clara Pueblo. Its Tewa name, *Ci-po-que*, means "place where the water cuts through." The village was originally named "Bove" by Juan de Oñate and then renamed "San Ildefonso" by him.

As was the fate of many other churches in the area, the original adobe church, founded around 1617 by Fray Cristóbal de Salazar, was destroyed in the 1680 Pueblo Revolt, and its two priests were killed. It was rebuilt in 1684 and almost immediately burned to the ground by the members of the pueblo in 1686. The replacement was not built until 1717 and lasted only fifty years, when it was considered irreparable and demolished, and another structure was built. The present church was built in 1968 on the site of the original church. It is in pueblo revival style with a choir loft and an exterior portal. The parapet high above the portal railing houses the bell; buttresses support the structure on each side.

The art contained in the church consists of several eighteenth-century oil paintings which were donated by the king of Spain when the church was rebuilt in 1717. Until recently, the main altar was comprised of a massive altar screen painted by contemporary Santa Fe santero Luis Tapia, but it was removed by the church elders in an attempt to "re-Indianize" the church.

The feast day is celebrated with Comanche and Buffalo Dances; a vesper procession is held the night before. The pueblo also holds a Matachines Dance on Christmas Day, in addition to a Corn Dance on June 13.

SAN ILDEFONSO
San Ildefonso Pueblo
FEAST DAYS: January 22 and 23

S A N T A   C L A R A

Santa Clara Pueblo

SANTA CLARA PUEBLO IS LOCATED AT THE FOOT of a mountain called the Sierra de Santa Clara on N.M. 30, 1 mile south of Española and about 27 miles from Santa Fe. Although historians believe the pueblo has been in existence since the early fourteenth century, it received its Spanish name from the colonizer Juan de Oñate in 1598. The Tewa name, *K'hapoo*, means "where roses grow near the water."

The original church was built in 1634 on the west bank of what is now called the Chama River but was destroyed in 1680 during the Pueblo Revolt. It was rebuilt in 1706 but later collapsed, and construction of the replacement was not begun until 1758 by the parish priest, Fray Mariano Rodriguez de la Torre. Since heavy vigas longer than 14 feet were unavailable for use as crossbeams, the church was a narrow structure 135 feet long. It withstood over a century of use until, in 1909, a pitched roof was added and the church collapsed under the weight. The current building was constructed of adobe in August 1918. It is in pueblo revival style and has a single tower with a bell. The interior has wood floors, and the ceiling is built of vigas and corbels with boards in between. The doors from the old church were hung on the new church, but after various remodelings they were replaced by modern ones.

There were two santero altar screens in the pre-1900 church, probably painted in the last quarter of the eighteenth century; however, these have long since disappeared, either having been destroyed when the church collapsed or removed prior to that time. The main altar is now comprised of small niches which house various depictions of the patron saint. The church was named for Saint Clare, founder of the Order of Saint Clares, an order of Franciscan cloistered nuns. According to legend, Saint Clare made clothing

SANTA CLARA
Santa Clara Pueblo
FEAST DAY: August 12

for Saint Francis of Assisi, and thus she is the patron saint of weavers and seamstresses.

The feast day is celebrated with various Indian dances, such as the Buffalo Dance or the Comanche Dance. On Christmas Day, a Matachines Dance is held at the pueblo, and on December 28, Holy Innocents Day is celebrated with children's dances.

SAN JOSÉ DE CHAMA

Hernández

*L*OCATED 6 MILES NORTH OF ESPAÑOLA ON THE road to Abiquiú, in the farming community of Hernández, this old adobe church is barely visible from the highway. Built in early 1850 by a private individual, it is in the cruciform plan and has a pitched corrugated metal roof with a belfry, both added in the 1950s. There are buttresses at the front with an extended arch opening above the parapet. It is reputed to have had three locally cast bells bearing the names of the donor's three daughters. The interior has wood floors, exposed vigas, and corbels. The graveyard is next to the churchyard.

Extensively remodeled in the 1950s, by 1970 the old church was no longer used for services, since a large modern church was constructed across the highway to accommodate the growing community. However, the old church is still used as a *morada* (meeting house) by members of the Penitente Brotherhood, who maintain it. The santero artwork from the old church has been moved to the new church, with the exception of an altar screen that has been loaned to a museum. This large altar screen, painted by Rafael Aragón, is now on long-term loan from the Archdiocese of Santa Fe to the Museum of International Folk Art in Santa Fe. The screen had suffered much water damage and whitewashing, and underwent considerable restoration during the 1970s at the Museum of International Folk Art.

The town of Hernández was immortalized by the famous Ansel Adams photograph "Moonrise at Hernandez," which has appeared in publications nationally. It captures the rising three-quarters moon amidst dramatic clouds above the Hernández cemetery with its white wooden crosses lit up by the last rays of the afternoon sun.

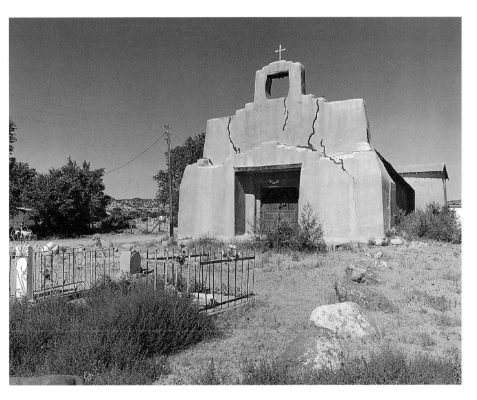

SAN JOSÉ DE CHAMA
Hernández
FEAST DAY: March 19

SAN FRANCISCO DE ASÍS

El Duende

*E*L DUENDE IS LOCATED 1/4 MILE PAST THE U.S. 84/ 285 junction. The village name means "the dwarf," indicating that it was considered tiny compared to other surrounding villages. The town is accessible by crossing the bridge from Chamita. The adobe church, built in 1896, has a corrugated metal pitched roof and a wooden belfry. In recent years a stone skirt has been added against the south wall. The interior has a viga ceiling and wood floors. The feast day is celebrated with a procession and a mass.

SAN FRANCISCO DE ASÍS
El Duende
FEAST DAY: October 4

SAN JUAN CABALLERO

San Juan Pueblo

SAN JUAN PUEBLO IS LOCATED 5 MILES NORTH OF Española, or approximately 29 miles north of Santa Fe just off N.M. 68. The original pueblo church was dedicated on September 8, 1598, after San Juan de los Caballeros was colonized by Juan de Oñate as the first permanent Spanish settlement in New Mexico and the capital of the province. Oñate brought with him 4,000 sheep, 1,000 goats, and 1,100 head of cattle, which heralded the beginning of the livestock industry in the colony. The church dedication celebration included a mock battle simulating Spain's conflict between Christian kings and invading Moors. This enactment undoubtedly made the Indians aware of the soldiers' capabilities.

The church survived for almost 100 years but was then destroyed in the Pueblo Revolt of 1680. In 1781, a smallpox epidemic took the lives of over one-third of the pueblo inhabitants. Almost a century later, in 1865, after the arrival of Archbishop Jean Baptiste Lamy in Santa Fe, a French priest, Camilo Seux, was assigned to the old adobe church at San Juan. Through his efforts, the eighteenth-century adobe structure was transformed: it was plastered, and a pitched roof, a spire, wooden floors, marble altars, and stained-glass windows were added.

In 1912, the church was demolished, and a new brick structure was built, an oddity surrounded as it was with adobe houses. It is in the cruciform plan with a metal-shingled roof and a bell tower; the interior has a vaulted ceiling and stained-glass windows.

There are no examples of santero folk art in this church. Since this art was one of the principal things Archbishop Lamy and the French priests disliked about northern New Mexico churches, one can assume that any examples that originally decorated this church were all burned or destroyed in other ways.

Across from the present church is a chapel built in 1890 by the same French priest and dedicated to Our Lady of Lourdes. It is constructed from cut stone similar to that used on the Loretto Chapel in Santa Fe, a red volcanic rock found west of the Río Grande.

The feast days of San Juan are celebrated on June 23 and June 24, with vespers and a Buffalo Dance on June 23 and races, chicken pulls, and a Comanche Dance on June 24. Other celebrations take place throughout the year at the pueblo: on Christmas Eve vespers are observed, and on Christmas Day a Matachines Dance is performed; on December 26 there is a Turtle Dance, and on June 13, a Corn Dance.

SAN JUAN CABALLERO

San Juan Pueblo

FEAST DAYS: June 23 and 24

SAN FRANCISCO DE ASÍS

Estaca

*E*STACA IS A SETTLEMENT NEAR ALCALDE ON THE
west side of the Río Grande. Its name means "stake." The village
is comprised of the small farms of fifteen to twenty families, who
grow wheat, corn, and other vegetables amidst apple orchards. The
adobe church was built in 1930. It has a pitched roof with a wooden
belfry; the entry porch is a later addition. The feast day is celebrated
with a mass and procession, followed by a village fiesta with music
and dances.

SAN FRANCISCO DE ASÍS
Estaca
FEAST DAY: October 4

SAN JOSÉ / SAN RAFAEL

El Guique

*L*OCATED 2 MILES NORTH OF SAN JUAN PUEBLO, the village of El Guique lies on the west bank of the Río Grande opposite the town of Alcalde. The church was built around 1900, even though the village had been established since the mid-1700s as San Rafael del Guique. It is constructed of adobe and has a metal pitched roof and wooden belfry. The interior has wood floors, and the ceiling beams have beaded edges.

SAN JOSÉ/SAN RAFAEL
El Guique
FEAST DAY: March 19

NUESTRA SEÑORA DE GUADALUPE

Velarde

*L*OCATED 14 MILES NORTHEAST OF ESPAÑOLA OFF N.M. 68, the village of Velarde was settled in the mid-1700s by the prominent Juan Antonio Perez Velarde family. It was formerly known as La Joya. Apple orchards became the major agricultural focus of the community and still are today, although many fine weavings have been made in Velarde.

The adobe church was built in 1817. The walls are 4 feet thick, and it has a corrugated metal pitched roof and a buttress at the rear. The belfry is a later addition. The interior has wood floors, vigas, corbels, and beams. There is a graveyard in the churchyard.

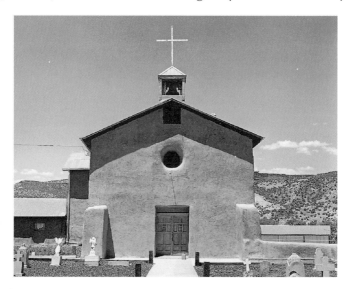

NUESTRA SEÑORA DE GUADALUPE
Velarde
FEAST DAY: December 12

LA CAPILLA DEL NACIMIENTO DEL NIÑO JESÚS

La Puebla

*L*OCATED ON A HILLSIDE 1/3 MILE SOUTH OF N.M. 76 and 1/2 mile east of the La Puebla turnoff, the church was built in 1876, as evidenced by a ceiling plank uncovered in recent restorations. It is of adobe construction with stone buttresses in front and has a corrugated metal pitched roof, which was a later addition. The interior has wood floors and vigas.

La Puebla was the birthplace of Francisco Martínez, who had followed in his father's footsteps as a maker of bells. He cast the bell for the church at Córdova which was named "María Antonio," and undoubtedly also cast the bell for this church. The feast day is celebrated on Christmas Eve at the conclusion of a novena which begins nine days before. On that day vespers are held, as well as a Matachines Dance in the afternoon, after which there is a procession.

LA CAPILLA DEL NACIMIENTO DEL NIÑO JESÚS

La Puebla

FEAST DAY: Christmas Eve

SANGRE DE CRISTO
Cuarteles
FEAST DAY: Good Friday

SANGRE DE CRISTO

Cuarteles

*L*OCATED SOUTH OF N.M. 76, 1 1/2 MILES EAST OF Santa Cruz Plaza, the church was built in 1849. Named after the surrounding Sangre de Cristo Mountains, it is of adobe construction with a corrugated metal pitched roof, wooden belfry, and wooden gable ends. The interior has wood floors and a pressed board ceiling covering the vigas.

The village of Cuarteles, a very old community established in the first quarter of the nineteenth century, is primarily a farming community, where such crops as corn, chile, and various varieties of fruit are grown. It is an extension of the village of Santa Cruz, established when villagers moved closer to the Río Grande for better farming. The acequias running through the community are still cleaned once each summer and blessed by the priest.

IGLESIA DE SANTA CRUZ
DE LA CAÑADA

Santa Cruz

SITUATED ON A HILL IN THE SANTA CRUZ VALLEY
overlooking a *villa* (town) which was once the center of the Spanish
colonial era, 2 miles east of Española on N.M. 76, this massive church
has survived over 250 years of continuous use. One of only three
existing churches in northern New Mexico at the time the Domínguez
survey was conducted in 1776, construction began after 1733 and
was completed by 1743. It is of adobe mud and mortar construction
in the cruciform plan, with a long nave and a steep gabled front;
it has twin bell towers with crosses and a cross above the parapet.
Massive buttresses support the back and sides. The pitched roof
was added in the early 1900s because of several severe storms in
prior years; it covers the clerestory, but the exposed vigas and corbels
still remain. The dirt floor was not covered until 1945, the same
year the stained-glass windows were installed. In preparation for
its 250th anniversary, there was considerable restoration of the
church, which included removal of hard-plaster from the interior
walls, which have now been mud-plastered by hand.

The interior is beautifully and dramatically furnished with
santero art dating back to 1765; several of these works were
documented in the Domínguez survey of 1776. The main altar screen,
probably constructed when the church was built, has been painted
and overpainted several times during the past two centuries by
various santeros. In the 1940s, it was painted by a parishioner in
stencil-like geometric designs, artwork which remained until 1983
when the various layers of overpainting were removed to expose
the floral and vine designs that can be seen currently. The altar
presently contains the work of two santeros, the upper portion
attributed to the Laguna Santero and the lower portion to

IGLESIA DE SANTA CRUZ DE LA CAÑADA
Santa Cruz
FEAST DAY: May 3

Rafael Aragón; this artwork surrounds centuries-old oil paintings which were donated by the king of Spain when the church was built. The magnificent Cristo at the center of the altar was carved by Rafael Aragón.

The large screen at the right side of the nave was painted by Rafael Aragón, probably after 1830. He painted over the original altar screen, which had been built and painted by the Laguna Santero at the beginning of the nineteenth century. Much of the original still remains below the overpainting, discovered by X-ray testing done in 1987.

The altar screen in the south chapel has also been overpainted in the last century. In 1985, the top layer (which had been painted by Rafael Aragón) was removed to expose a layer by Pedro Antonio

Fresquís (not previously known to have painted an altar screen outside of Truchas and Chamita). On several panels the Fresquís layer was removed to expose the bottom layer, which had been painted by the Laguna Santero. The altar screen now contains examples of work by both these early santeros, the top layer having been completely removed.

There are several other magnificent examples of santero art in the church, including a Christ in the Tomb (El Santo Entierro) which dates to approximately 1776 and a life-size standing Christ figure (Nuestro Padre Jesús Nazareno).

Since the early 1900s the Sons of the Holy Family, an order of priests that originated in Spain, has been in charge of the church. At one time its missions included the Indian pueblos of Santa Clara, San Ildefonso, Pojoaque, and Nambé. The Dominican convent next door opened in 1928, and the sisters took charge of the elementary school.

For many years, Santa Cruz residents have presented the folk drama of *Los Moros y Los Cristianos* (*The Moors and the Christians*), a production entirely on horseback representing a battle between the Moors and the Christian Spaniards. This play was sometimes presented on the feast day of Our Lady of Carmel, July 16, and also on Santa Cruz Day, May 3.

For the 250th anniversary celebration, the Restoration Committee published a book about the history, legends, and artwork of the church entitled, *La Iglesia de Santa Cruz de La Cañada, 1733–1983*; it is available for sale in the church.

The feast day is celebrated with festivities which include a Matachines Dance.

S A N　　　I S I D R O

La Mesilla

*T*HE VILLAGE OF LA MESILLA, WHICH MEANS "little table," is located 3 miles south of U.S. 285. The town is an extension of the village of Santa Cruz, having been established by farmers who wished to be closer to the Río Grande. The adobe church was built in 1918. It has a corrugated metal pitched roof and wooden belfry. The interior has wood floors and a flat pressboard ceiling. During the feast day the bulto of the patron saint, Saint Isidore the Farmer (San Isidro Labrador), is carried in procession to bless the fields and crops.

SAN ISIDRO
La Mesilla
FEAST DAY: May 15

CHAPTER THREE

Along The High Road To Taos

ALONG THE HIGH ROAD TO TAOS *there is an unusually high concentration of historic churches, many with colorful graveyards. This popular route begins about 16 miles north of Santa Fe, where N.M. 503 turns east just beyond the turnoff to Los Alamos. This road and N.M. 75, 76, and 518 have come to be called the High Road to Taos. The numerous churches in this area are situated amidst charming historic villages, most of which were founded in the eighteenth century on land grants; the people of these villages have preserved their old religious and social customs, so that life here today is still reminiscent of life over 200 years ago. The variety of landscape in the region also adds to its appeal: it ranges from fertile farmlands punctuated by giant cottonwood trees that turn golden in autumn to heavily forested alpine areas whose peaks are snowcapped in winter.*

When touring this area, make plans to spend at least a half hour at each historic church, beginning at Nambé. The smaller churches, such as those at Cundiyó, Ojo Sarco, and Río Lucío can usually only be viewed from the exterior, since it is likely they will not be open. At Córdova, Truchas, and Las Trampas, inquiry can sometimes be made of villagers as to when the church might be open. Upon reaching Picurís Pueblo, it is advisable to read the posted rules regarding entry to pueblo lands. In the Peñasco area, after viewing the missions, a drive through nearby Santa Bárbara Canyon is a wonderful experience any time of year.

After completing the tour, the fastest road back to Santa Fe is the highway through Dixon, which will return you to the Old Taos Highway and to Santa Fe without having to retrace the route just taken through the villages.

SAGRADO CORAZÓN

Nambé

ALSO IN THE VILLAGE OF NAMBÉ, ON N.M. 503, IS the church of Sagrado Corazón (Sacred Heart). Built on a hill next to the highway in 1947 after the original church burned, it is of adobe construction in the pueblo revival style, designed by architect Urban Weidner. It has twin bell towers with crosses on top, pilasters along the exterior nave walls, stained-glass windows, and a covered clerestory window. The interior is painted plaster, and it has wood floors, vigas, corbels, and wood-paneled doors. Tin light fixtures made during the revival period hang from the ceiling. The feast day is celebrated with a mass and traditional Indian dances.

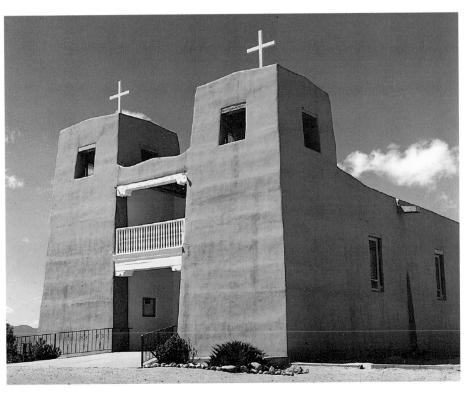

SAGRADO CORAZÓN
Nambé
FEAST DAY: October 4

SAN FRANCISCO DE ASÍS

Nambé Pueblo

NAMBÉ PUEBLO IS A TEWA-SPEAKING INDIAN pueblo about 21 miles from Santa Fe, 4 miles from U.S. 285 on N.M. 503. Its Tewa name, *Nambay-onghwee*, translates to "people of the roundish earth." Surrounded by mountains and near the Nambé River, the church, built in 1725, is a replacement for an earlier one which was gutted in the 1680 and 1696 pueblo uprisings. The 1725 church, in use until it collapsed in August 1908 during a severe storm, contained a crossbeam which reads: "The Lord Governor Don Juan Domingo Bustamante built this church at his own expense in 1725." The old church was condemned in 1960, and the present church, designed by architect Allan McKnown, was built in 1974, within 100 feet of the site of the original church. The bell from the original church hangs above the doorway. Several of the eighteenth-century beams, including the inscribed beam mentioned above, along with a panel from an altar screen painted by Bernardo Miera y Pacheco, one of the earliest known of the eighteenth-century New Mexican santeros, are now incorporated into the Gerald and Ina Sizer Cassidy house in Santa Fe. Few examples of santero art remain in the church.

The feast day is celebrated on October 4 with various Indian dances performed at the pueblo. On July 4, the Nambé Falls Ceremony is held.

SAN FRANCISCO DE ASÍS

Nambé Pueblo

FEAST DAY: October 4

S A N T O D O M I N G O

Cundiyó

*L*OCATED OFF N.M. 503, THE VILLAGE OF CUNDIYÓ was founded in the late 1700s by Captain José Antonio Vigil, who received a land grant prior to the completion of his tour of duty in the army. Vigil's ancestors still occupy homes there since the land grant has remained in the family, even though it has been divided many times. The village was named by Tewa-speaking Indians and means "the round hill of the little bells." Tales of buried treasure near the village, at Cerro de la Patada, abounded for many years. The people of Cundiyó, especially the young men, would spend time in church praying they would find the bars of gold and silver and the other items lost when a caravan was attacked by Indians; many of the villagers searched in vain for the two peach trees between which the treasure was supposed to have been buried.

The adobe church was built in 1838. It has a pitched corrugated metal roof. There is a handmade wooden cross on top of the wooden belfry, and the interior has wood floors and a sheetrock ceiling. To the north of the church lies the graveyard.

SANTO DOMINGO
Cundiyó
FEAST DAY: August 4

SANTUARIO DE CHIMAYÓ

Chimayó

BECAUSE IT IS BELIEVED THAT THIS CHURCH WAS built upon sacred earth that has miraculous healing powers, the Santuario de Chimayó is visited perhaps more than any of the northern chapels. Situated in Chimayó (9 miles east of Española on N.M. 76), which was settled by Spaniards prior to 1680 and resettled in 1695 at the foothills of the Sangre de Cristo Mountains, the Santuario is surrounded by a variety of tall trees which shade it from the summer sun. Built originally as a private chapel by Don Bernardo Abeyta around 1814, the church is 60 feet long and 24 feet wide, with adobe walls close to 40 inches thick. The pitched corrugated metal roof was added during World War I. It has a buttress at the rear, and twin towers with a bell and a parapet in the attic. The interior is mud-plastered and painted, and the ceiling contains vigas with corbels and carved, broad beams. The entry has a flagstone floor.

Abeyta commissioned several santeros to paint altar screens and carve bultos to adorn the interior of the church, magnificent works which remain to this day as a tribute to his generosity. The santero Molleno painted the main altar screen and carved the large crucifix at its base; later he painted the altar screen to the right. José Aragón painted the two altar screens on the left around 1820; Rafael Aragón carved the bulto of Saint Raphael the Archangel (San Rafael Arcángel), which sits in the niche of the first altar screen on the left, as well as the second altar screen on the right closest to the altar. Other fine examples of santero art adorn the church, including a carved image of Saint James (Santiago), patron saint of horsemen. The original doors of the church, carved and inscribed in 1816 by Pedro Domínguez, are still in use.

After Abeyta's death, the church was left to his daughter, Carmen

SANTUARIO DE CHIMAYÓ
Chimayó
FEAST DAYS: January 15 and July 25

Chávez, who maintained it in immaculate condition for many years, welcoming all who came searching for a miracle. In 1929, it was sold to several residents of Santa Fe, among them Mary Austin and John Gaw Meem, who raised needed funds and who eventually turned it over to the Archdiocese of Santa Fe. The church was designated a National Historic Site in 1970.

During Holy Week thousands of people walk to the Santuario from places near and far, many arriving on Good Friday. The healing earth is contained in a small pit in the floor of the chapel dedicated to Saint Raphael the Archangel in the room to the left of the main altar. For over 150 years it has been the practice of pilgrims to take a small quantity of the healing earth with them when they leave; and hundreds of people who have been healed by their visit to this shrine have left their crutches and braces to hang on the walls of the room. Every year scores of these implements are removed and placed in storage, only to be replaced by the many more left by faithful believers.

The gift shop next to the church sells local crafts, as well as booklets describing the intriguing history of the church and the legends surrounding the Cristo around which the church was originally built. The plaza surrounding the church consists of many picturesque old adobe structures. Nearby, there is a nineteenth-century private chapel dedicated to Saint Bonaventure (San Buenaventura), built by the Ortega family of Chimayó. According to an inscription on the ceiling, it dates from 1873, and it is still maintained much as it was in the last century. Holy Family, the modern parish church, is located nearby.

The feast of Our Lord of Esquípulas (Nuestro Señor de Esquípulas) is celebrated on January 15. In addition, each year on the weekend closest to July 25, the feast day of Saint James (Santiago) is celebrated with various religious and social events. During the weekend a play entitled *Los Moros y Los Cristianos* (*The Moors and the Christians*) is performed, to the great delight of both residents and visitors.

SAN ANTONIO DE PADUA

Córdova

THIS VILLAGE WAS ORIGINALLY NAMED SAN FRANcisco Xavier de Pueblo Quemado, but its name was changed to Córdova in 1925 when the post office was established. Córdova is noted for the many wood-carvers who have lived there since the 1850s, the most famous of which was José Dolores López (1868–1937), whose family still continues the tradition of making finely sanded unpainted wood carvings with incised designs. The best-known members of the López family are his son, George, and his granddaughter, Gloria López Córdova, whose workshop is in the center of the village and is visited by people from all areas. Other relatives of the elder López still practice this craft in the village.

Nestled in the center of the residential district of Córdova, on the High Road to Taos, 14 miles east of Española and a short distance from N.M. 76, the church is surrounded by adobe houses as old as the church itself. It is kept locked except during services. It was built in the early 1830s, licensed as a public chapel, and paid for by Don Bernardo Abeyta, the same donor who built the Santuario de Chimayó. The church is of adobe construction with a pitched corrugated metal roof added in the 1940s. It has a bell tower with an old bell. The interior has wood floors, a balcony at the rear, which was originally used as a choir loft, and a board ceiling with vigas and corbels. The structure has remained virtually the same since 1925 when an interior buttress, which resembles a long shelf, was added on the right-hand side of the church to combat water seepage.

The interior is decorated with a large main altar screen painted in the 1830s by Rafael Aragón, flanked by two smaller altar screens also painted by him. Other fine examples of nineteenth-century santero art also adorn the church, most having survived from the time the church was built, due to the diligent caretaking of the mayordomos.

The feast day is celebrated with a mass and procession in which all the parishioners as well as visitors participate.

SAN ANTONIO DE PADUA
Córdova
FEAST DAY: June 16

NUESTRA SEÑORA DEL ROSARIO

Truchas

*F*ARTHER NORTH ON THE HIGH ROAD TO TAOS, situated on a long level ridge of the Sangre de Cristo Mountains, 44 miles from Santa Fe off N.M. 76, the old adobe church in Truchas has survived the ravages of many harsh winters. The Spanish name of the village means "trout," most likely so named because of the nearby stream, Truchas Creek, once a popular fishing area. Although the community of Truchas was established in 1754 as a land grant settlement for the Romero families of Santa Cruz and the Espinosa families and others of Chimayó, the church was not built until sometime after the beginning of the nineteenth century. Enclosed in a walled yard, the church is hard-plastered, and an inscription on the ceiling indicates it was reroofed in 1878, after the collapse of its eastern facade and tower. The corrugated metal roof was added around 1900. It has a bell tower with louvered openings, a circular attic window, double-hung wood windows with shutters, and a buttress on the south side. The interior has plastered and painted walls, wood floors, and a ceiling composed of vigas and corbels.

The church contains two altar screens, a large main screen and a small side screen, both magnificent examples of dated work by the santero Pedro Antonio Fresquís, and both with inscriptions in his hand. The inscription on the large screen refers to the Blessed Virgin, and the one on the small screen indicates that it was completed on July 3, 1821, and paid for by Gregorio Sandobal. There are also other fine examples of santero art in the church, much of it dating from the time the church was built, its survival due to the scrupulous preservation practices of the mayordomos. Longtime Truchas residents Susie Romero and her mother, Carmelita, have worked diligently to generate interest among the parishioners for keeping the old church in good condition, arranging

NUESTRA SEÑORA DEL ROSARIO
Truchas
FEAST DAY: October 7

for reroofing and replastering, as well as providing security measures.

Several miles away, on the road leading out of the village, a new church was built in the 1970s, but the old church is still maintained by the members of the Altar Society, the Carmelitas. Holy Week services are still conducted at the old church, which is situated in the center of the village, surrounded by the old adobe houses of the parishioners who have attended services here for many years. The feast day is celebrated with vespers, a mass, and a procession.

S A N T O T O M Á S

Ojo Sarco

*L*OCATED OFF N.M. 76 ON THE HIGH ROAD TO TAOS, 6 miles north of Truchas, the village of Ojo Sarco is comprised of a cluster of farms along a tiny stream by the same name, which means "clear spring." Most of the village structures are strung out along two side roads which meet 2 miles west of the highway.

The adobe church was built in 1886. It has a pitched metal corrugated roof and wood siding at its gables. The original wood doors are still being used. The interior has vigas and wood flooring, and the original altar rail, still extant, is of latticed wood. The feast day is celebrated with a procession through the dirt roads of the valley during which the santos are carried by parishioners so that the patron saint, Saint Thomas (Santo Tomás) may bless the acequias, the fields, and the animals to ensure prosperous crops and livestock.

SANTO TOMÁS
Ojo Sarco
FEAST DAY: July 3

SAN JOSÉ DE GRACIA DE LAS TRAMPAS
Las Trampas
FEAST DAY: March 19

SAN JOSÉ DE GRACIA
DE LAS TRAMPAS

Las Trampas

*T*HE VILLAGE OF LAS TRAMPAS WAS SETTLED IN 1754 by seventy-four-year-old Juan de Arguello and a dozen or so families. It is located 22 miles south of Taos on N.M. 76 but is also accessible from Santa Fe on the High Road to Taos. The village name means "the traps, or snares"—items used by the early trappers who traded animal hides to settlers in this area. There is also a legend about the name of the village which relates that in the early days of the settlement when raiding Indians would approach the village, an old man and woman would appear, angrily waving clubs to drive them off; thus intruders would consider the village "a trap."

At the time that Las Trampas was originally settled, the closest church was 9 miles away at Picurís Pueblo. In order to finance the construction of their own church, the villagers collected one-sixth of each family's meager earnings from their crops. All the work was done by the villagers themselves, and it was finally completed in 1760. The church is listed in the Domínguez survey of 1776. Other than Holy Cross Church at Santa Cruz and San Miguel Church at Santa Fe, this is the only northern church remaining which dates from the eighteenth century; all others were constructed after 1776.

Originally named Santo Tomás del Río de las Trampas, the church is still in use after more than 225 years. It is of adobe construction with a hand-plastered mud exterior. It is in the cruciform style and has two towers, wooden belfries, and an exterior balcony used when processions moved outside the church and the choir would continue to sing on the balcony. The interior has wood floors, a handcarved nineteenth-century wooden pulpit, a latticed altar rail, and a choir loft rail. The ceiling, with vigas and corbels, is painted with eighteenth- and nineteenth-century designs throughout, with a clerestory window above the beginning of the painted ceiling. It is said that the original bells which hung in the twin towers were made of gold and silver mixed with less precious metals and that one bell, named "María del Refugio," was rung for masses for the dead or for the death of an adult; the other bell, named "María de la Gracia," had a gentler tone and was rung for mass and for the death of infants. "Gracia" is the only bell which remains now.

The interior of the church is decorated with the work of eighteenth- and nineteenth-century santeros. There are eight altar screens in the church. The main altar screen was probably built and painted in the early 1800s by another santero, but it was overpainted in 1860 by the Mexican santero José de Gracia Gonzales, who also overpainted the remaining screens. Several of the santos gracing the altars date as far back as 1776 and are attributed to the santero Bernardo Miera y Pacheco. The remaining santos are additional examples of the folk art of the era.

The Society for the Preservation of New Mexico Mission Churches was responsible for reroofing the church in 1932, and it was designated a National Historic Site in 1967 when it was restored completely to its original state. The parishioners periodically join forces to maintain the church, remudding the structure every two to three years. These parishioners, as well as the mayordomos, have received national recognition for their efforts to maintain and preserve their historic church.

The church is generally kept locked except during services and feast days. The feast day is celebrated with vespers, a procession, a mass, and other festivities which continue throughout the day.

SAGRADO CORAZÓN

Río Lucío

*L*OCATED 1 1/2 MILES WEST OF N.M. 76 ON N.M. 75 near Peñasco, the village is adjacent to Carson National Forest and Picurís Pueblo. It is a small farming community that cultivates primarily high-altitude crops such as corn, peas, and alfalfa, along with apples. The adobe church was built in 1920. It has a corrugated metal pitched roof and wooden belfry. The interior has wood floors and vigas.

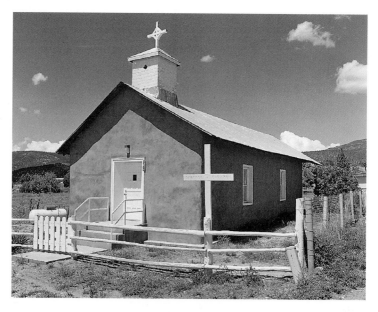

SAGRADO CORAZÓN
Río Lucío
FEAST DAY: May 3

SAN LORENZO DE PICURÍS

Picurís Pueblo

*T*HIS INDIAN SETTLEMENT IS LOCATED ABOUT 46 miles from Santa Fe and about 20 miles from Taos, off the High Road to Taos on N.M. 75; it is also accessible from N.M. 68. The church at this pueblo has been rebuilt numerous times since the mid-1500s. During the Pueblo Revolt of 1680, the priest was murdered, and the existing church was burned to the ground. The village was abandoned for several years, and a new church was not built until 1746, only to be destroyed by raiding Comanche Indians in 1769. Sometime after 1776 the church was again rebuilt, not of adobe bricks but of puddled adobe, mud poured into molds, a method used at Casas Grandes in Arizona and at other ancient Indian sites. Later, in 1900, a pitched roof was added, which remained on the structure until 1960, when the church was almost entirely rebuilt once again.

The church collapsed completely in 1986, and in May of 1987, it was leveled due to irreparable cracks in the walls caused by water seepage; it was then reconstructed again in 1988 using the same floor plan and exterior style as the 1770s church. Sixteen thousand adobes were made near the church and then laid, enough to re-construct half of the walls; later, another 16,000 were made to complete the structure. New doors, windows, and vigas were installed, and only a few of the old corbels were used. Most of the work was done by volunteers from or near the community, with the aid of numerous volunteers from elsewhere in New Mexico and around the nation, including a motorcycle club from Santa Fe. Prior to its reconstruction, the church had been one of the four remaining northern churches listed in the Domínguez survey of 1776. Today, only the original entrance to the church remains as it did in the eighteenth century.

SAN LORENZO DE PICURÍS
Picurís Pueblo
FEAST DAYS: August 9 and 10

The church is furnished with art of the early santeros, including a large altar screen painted around 1820 by Rafael Aragón. The top center panel of the altar screen is a painting of Our Lady of Guadalupe (Nuestra Señora de Guadalupe) on canvas painted by Aragón over an old canvas which had been in the church for many years. The altar screen panels surround an oil painting of Saint Lawrence (San Lorenzo) which was donated by the king of Spain to the church in the 1700s.

The feast days are celebrated on August 9 and 10 with a Sunset Dance performed on August 9 and various dances, pole climbing, and footraces held on August 10. The feast day coincides with the 1680 Pueblo Revolt, which occurred on the feast day of Saint Lawrence. On Christmas Eve vespers are held, and a Matachines Dance is performed on Christmas Day.

S A N   A C A C I O

Llano Largo

*L*OCATED ABOUT 2 MILES FROM PEÑASCO, THE village of Llano Largo is near the Santa Bárbara Campground by the river of the same name in the Carson National Forest. The adobe church was built in 1936. It has a corrugated metal roof and wooden belfry. The interior has wood floors and a viga and latilla ceiling; it contains a small altar screen dating from the 1860s by the santero José de Gracia Gonzales, which, however, must have been brought from another location since it is older than the construction date of the church.

SAN ACACIO
Llano Largo
FEAST DAY: June 22

SAN JUAN NEPOMUCENO

Llano San Juan

*L*OCATED OFF N.M. 76 IN THE PEÑASCO AREA, THE village, which is adjacent to Carson National Forest, was founded in 1796 by three families who petitioned Governor Fernando Chacón for permission to build several towns in the valley. The residents were farmers, raising fruits, vegetables, sheep, and cattle primarily for their own use.

The adobe church was built around 1832. It is mud-plastered and has a corrugated metal pitched roof and belfry, both of which were added later. There is a stone buttress at the rear corner. The interior has wood flooring, and the ceiling vigas are covered. There is a graveyard next to the church.

SAN JUAN NEPOMUCENO
Llano San Juan
FEAST DAY: May 16

CHAPTER FOUR

The Abiquiú Area

THE ABIQUIÚ AREA, *in the heart of the Chama River Valley, has come to be known as Georgia O'Keeffe country because the painter lived and worked there from about 1943 until just before her death in 1986. The region abounds with striking multicolored cliffs and mesas, which provided inspiration for many of her paintings. In addition to the numerous historic churches in this area, there is the unusual geological formation known as Echo Amphitheater, where children and adults alike enjoy shouting into the canyon walls and getting an eerie response. Also located in the area is Ghost Ranch, where O'Keeffe once lived, now owned by the United Presbyterian Church and used as an educational facility and conference center. The National Forest Service maintains the Ghost Ranch Living Museum near the highway, a free public museum which has exhibits of Indian artifacts, dinosaur fossils, and live animals native to the region.*

When touring the churches of the area, the first stop should be at the historic church at Abiquiú, Santo Tomás. Many of the smaller communities around Abiquiú may not always be accessible during wet or snowy weather. It may be necessary to consult a current road map to determine which roads are dirt roads more easily traveled by four-wheel drive vehicles and to more accurately determine the distance between villages. If time is a factor, instead of attempting to cross over from the Los Ojos area to the Vallecitos Valley and down through El Rito, this area may also be reached by returning to Abiquiú, traveling to the turnoff at Ojo Caliente, and then up through La Madera and Vallecitos, also a picturesque drive through heavily forested areas.

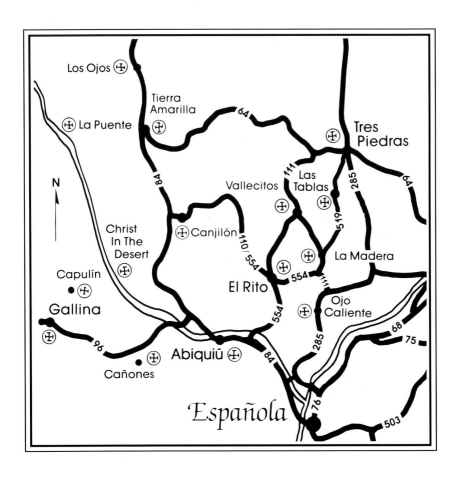

SANTO TOMÁS DE ABIQUIÚ

Abiquiú

*T*HE VILLAGE OF ABIQUIÚ IS LOCATED 18 MILES northwest of Española on U.S. 84. It was settled in the 1740s for *genízaros* (converted Indians who had lost their tribal identity) and quickly became an important trade and defense center due to its location along the northwestern edge of Spanish civilization. Trading commenced with the Navajo and Ute tribes that roamed the entire New Mexican frontier. The original settlers raised sheep and cattle.

Abiquiú is associated with several well-known people. It is the birthplace of the famous and sometimes controversial priest Padre Antonio José Martínez of Taos, who in the period from 1830–1867 singlehandedly and tirelessly worked to bring progress to northern New Mexico. Among his contributions were the purchase of the first printing press in New Mexico in 1835. In addition, famous painter Georgia O'Keeffe adopted Abiquiú as her home and lived and painted there from about 1943 until just before her death in 1986.

The church at Abiquiú has had two patron saints: Saint Rose of Lima (Santa Rosa de Lima), patroness of the church built in 1744, and Saint Thomas (Santo Tomás), patron of the church which was built around 1773. The feast days of both saints are still observed today. Santo Tomás de Abiquiú survived until 1867 when it was destroyed in a fire caused by a candle lit by a parishioner at the altar. Today, only a 12-foot adobe wall is visible 1 1/2 miles east of Abiquiú on U.S. 84. The people of Abiquiú rebuilt their church, but by 1930 it was in a state of disrepair. Famed architect John Gaw Meem, long a supporter of the preservation of historic churches, provided plans for the new church to be named Santo Tomás de Abiquiú, and construction of the new building began after Holy

SANTO TOMÁS DE ABIQUIÚ
Abiquiú
FEAST DAYS: July 3 and August 23

Week in 1937. The parishioners provided the labor and 48,000 adobes, and the Society for the Preservation of New Mexico Mission Churches provided most of the other building materials.

The adobe structure is in the cruciform plan and has a flat built-up roof. It has a portal and a balcony with a bell in the arched opening above the parapet; there are buttresses at the front and along the nave, and the windows are double-hung. The interior has a wood floor covered with linoleum, and the ceiling is of vigas and corbels. There is a clerestory window and a choir loft.

The feast days are celebrated on July 3 (Saint Thomas) and August 23 (Saint Rose of Lima), with vespers, a mass, a procession, and other festivities attended by the entire community.

S A N M I G U E L

Cañones

*L*OCATED ON N.M. 96, 7 MILES WEST OF ABIQUIÚ, this small mountain village was settled in 1818. It is surrounded by ponderosa pine forests of the San Pedro and San Juan mountains. Much of this area is inaccessible during the snowy winter months. The adobe church was built in 1859. It has a corrugated metal pitched roof and a bell tower to the left of the entry. The walls are mud-plastered annually by the parishioners. The interior has wood floors and vigas.

SAN MIGUEL
Cañones
FEAST DAY: September 29

S A N T O N I Ñ O

Capulín

T HE VILLAGE OF CAPULÍN, WHICH MEANS "CHOKE-cherry," is located in the Santa Fe National Forest near Abiquiú. Established in the late 1870s, the town was originally named Sedman (in honor of the superintendent of the Atchison, Topeka and Santa Fe Railroad), but had been changed to Capulín by the turn of the century. The adobe church was built around 1920. It has a corrugated metal pitched roof with a separate wooden bell tower built a few feet from the church. The feast day of the Child Jesus (Santo Niño) is celebrated on a day chosen by the parishioners, with vespers, a mass, and a procession.

SANTO NIÑO
Capulín
FEAST DAY: date varies

NUESTRA SEÑORA DE GUADALUPE

Gallina

*L*OCATED ON N.M. 96, APPROXIMATELY 40 MILES
from Abiquiú, the village of Gallina is bounded by the Santa Fe
National Forest. Its name means "hen," probably referring to the
wild fowl found in the area. In a pastoral setting, the village is
surrounded by grassy meadows scattered with cattle. The adobe
church was built around 1954. It has a corrugated metal pitched
roof and a wooden belfry. Although the village was settled in 1818
by Antonio Ortiz, because of its close proximity to Abiquiú, the
villagers did not need their own church until the mid-twentieth
century.

NUESTRA SEÑORA DE GUADALUPE
Gallina
FEAST DAY: December 12

CHRIST IN THE DESERT MONASTERY

Abiquiú

NESTLED IN THE CHAMA CANYON APPROXI-
mately 13 miles north of Abiquiú off N.M. 84 on a dirt road, the
monastery was built in 1964. It was founded by Father Aelred Wall
and other Benedictine monks from the Mount Saviour Monastery
in New York State. It exists to "sing God's praises in the wilderness."
The monastery provides retreats for interested persons, and the
Benedictine Brothers run a gift shop, the proceeds from which are
used for maintaining the premises. Depending on the size of the
building fund at any given time, the structure is being periodically
enlarged and remodeled.

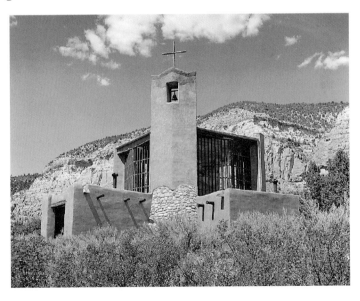

CHRIST IN THE DESERT MONASTERY
Abiquiú
FEAST DAY: none

SAN JUAN NEPOMUCENO

Canjilón

*T*HE VILLAGE OF CANJILÓN IS LOCATED JUST OFF
U.S. 84 on N.M. 115. Although some historians indicate the area
was settled in the late 1770s, the adobe church was not built until
1878. The oldest church in the Tierra Amarilla area, it is in the
cruciform plan with a pitched roof. Although use of it was dis-
continued in 1972 when the new church was built nearby, the New
Mexico Community Foundation, along with the local community,
has undertaken restoration of the historic building. Among other
renovations, shoring was installed to stabilize the building and
prevent further collapse of the ceiling.

SAN JUAN NEPOMUCENO
Canjilón
FEAST DAY: May 16

S A N   M I G U E L

La Puente

$\mathcal{T}$HE VILLAGE OF LA PUENTE, WHICH MEANS "THE bridge," is located in the Tierra Amarilla area on N.M. 531. The old adobe church burned in 1900, and a new one, constructed of adobes made by villagers, was built in 1914. It is in the cruciform plan, with a corrugated metal pitched roof. The villagers, who resettled from Tierra Azul, a town near Abiquiú, venerated Saint Michael the Archangel (San Miguel Arcángel) and thus named the church in his honor.

SAN MIGUEL
La Puente
FEAST DAY: September 29

S A N   J O S É

Los Ojos

*L*OS OJOS IS LOCATED IN THE TIERRA AMARILLA
area 1/2 mile south of the N.M. 95/84 junction, and although
established around 1860 as part of the original Tierra Amarilla
land grant, it did not become a parish until January 1883, when
it consisted of as many as twenty villages. The church was completed
by the end of the same year; it has two chapels attached to the
front, one dedicated to Saint Francis of Assisi (San Francisco de
Asís) and the other to Saint Clare (Santa Clara). Prior to that time,
services were held either in private homes or in the oratories of
the Penitente Brotherhood.

In 1930, the church was demolished, and the parishioners began
to rebuild it, making 105,000 adobe bricks; however, the adobes
remained stacked until 1935 when the villagers continued with the
reconstruction, which was completed in 1950. Stained-glass windows
from an earlier remodeling of the old church were installed in the
new church.

According to publications, the feast of Saint Joseph (San José)
is celebrated on October 22 instead of March 19; but the important
feast days celebrated in the community are those of Saint James
(Santiago) and Saint Anne (Santa Ana), celebrated on July 25 and 26.

SAN JOSÉ
Los Ojos
FEAST DAYS: July 25, 26, and October 22

S A N T O N I Ñ O

Tierra Amarilla

*I*N 1880, THE COUNTY SEAT OF RÍO ARRIBA COUNTY was moved to Nutritas, and the name of this village was changed to Tierra Amarilla; it was settled by former residents of Abiquiú and surrounding areas. Although the village did not yet have a church when first established, the first baptism was performed there in April 1862 by priests from Abiquiú. In 1869, Tierra Amarilla was transferred to the El Rito Parish, but the church was not constructed until 1907. It is of adobe construction with walls ranging in size from 2 feet to 6 feet; it has a pitched roof with a bell tower. The interior is in the cruciform plan, and the windows are constructed in a neo-Gothic style. The feast day is celebrated on a day chosen by the priest and parishioners, with vespers, a mass, and a procession.

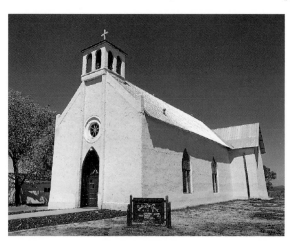

SANTO NIÑO
Tierra Amarilla
FEAST DAY: date varies

CONCEPCIÓN INMACULADA

Tres Piedras

*T*HIS LUMBER AND RANCHING COMMUNITY IS located 35 miles northwest of Taos on U.S. 285. Tres Piedras ("three rocks") is so named because of the three massive granite boulders which can be seen from many miles away. The village was settled in 1879, but the adobe church was not built until 1900. It has a corrugated metal pitched roof, wooden belfry, and gable ends. The windows are constructed in a neo-Gothic style. The interior has vigas and a tongue-and-groove wood floor.

CONCEPCIÓN INMACULADA
Tres Piedras
FEAST DAY: December 8

SAN LUIS GONZALO DE AMARANTE

Las Tablas

*T*HIS MUD-PLASTERED ADOBE CHURCH, LOCATED in the village of Las Tablas (meaning "the boards") on N.M. 519, 5 miles from Petaca, was built in 1899. It has a corrugated metal pitched roof, wooden belfry, and vigas, which were added in the 1930s. The interior has wood floors and square-cut vigas. There is a graveyard in the churchyard. Although the correct name of the patron saint of this church is Saint Amarant of Gonzaga (San Amarante de Gonzaga), due to local usage, the church's name remains San Luis Gonzalo.

SAN LUIS GONZALO DE AMARANTE
Las Tablas
FEAST DAY: June 21

NUESTRA SEÑORA DE GUADALUPE

La Madera

*L*OCATED AT THE FORK OF N.M. 519/111, LA MADERA was settled in 1820 by Juan de Díos Chacón. For many years the village was the center of a large sawmill operation; consequently, its name means "lumber," or "wood." The adobe church was built in 1918. It has a trapezoidal apse, a corrugated metal pitched roof, and a wooden belfry with a bell. The interior has a tile ceiling over a coved ceiling, wood floors, and a choir loft. It contains a contemporary altar screen and Cristo carved and painted by santeros Zoraida and Eulogio Ortega of Velarde.

NUESTRA SEÑORA DE GUADALUPE
La Madera
FEAST DAY: December 12

NUESTRA SEÑORA DE LOS DOLORES

Vallecitos

*L*OCATED OFF N.M. 111 IN THE OJO CALIENTE AREA, the adobe church was built in 1880, even though the village had been established a century earlier. The villagers apparently attended services at the nearby El Rito church until their own church was built. It has a corrugated metal pitched roof, wood-shingle belfry, and gable ends, all added later. The interior has wood floors and vigas. Saint Turbius of Mogrobejo (Santo Toribio) was the patron saint to the 1770s families of Lower Vallecito, while Saint Anthony of Padua (San Antonio de Padua) was the patron saint of the later village of Upper Vallecito.

NUESTRA SEÑORA DE LOS DOLORES
Vallecitos
FEAST DAY: September 15

SAN JUAN NEPOMUCENO

El Rito

E L RITO IS A RANCHING COMMUNITY, WHOSE main industry was sheepraising; it is located at the end of N.M. 554, 26 miles north of Española, off the road to Abiquiú (U.S. 84). The community originally had two grist mills which have since disappeared. Construction of the massive church was begun around 1827 and completed in 1832. The floor plan was the cruciform type, and with its 5-foot-thick adobe walls and 120-foot length, the church could be used as a fortress. It has magnificent carved vigas and corbels, with an inscription on the viga below the clerestory: *"Ce yso esta fabryca el año de 1832."* "This [building] was made in the year 1832." (This loosely translates to: "This church was completed in 1832.")

In 1869, after the arrival of the French priests in northern New Mexico, the parish seat was moved from Abiquiú to El Rito, and San Juan Nepomuceno became a mother church, occupied by French priests for fifty-five years. Shortly thereafter, the adobe church was remodeled according to French influence. In 1876, a pitched roof was added, and the clerestory window was covered. Moreover, the front wall of the church was replaced in a style different from the rest of the building. In 1905, a new bell was installed, and its resonant sound could be heard for a 12-mile radius calling the parishioners to worship.

In 1915, the main altar screen containing nine panels which had survived for almost a century, was removed. Its location remains a mystery; it is not known whether it was sold or destroyed. The wall behind the altar was torn out, and a French stained-glass window was put in. In addition, the earthen floor was covered with wood, and many plaster of paris statues were installed to replace the old santos. The corrugated tin pitched roof was added in 1925. In the

1940s, hard-plaster instead of mud-plaster was applied to the exterior walls.

By 1979, the deterioration of the building was evident, and in September of that year the interior walls of the nave collapsed. The reconstruction, undertaken by Father Jerome Martínez y Alire and his parishioners, took several years. Seemingly insurmountable problems were encountered: the new walls collapsed, requiring their removal; it was necessary to change contractors; and new steel framework was required before reconstruction could begin again.

Because of the unforeseen problems and the length of time required for reconstruction, services were held in the interim at various places, first at the local morada and then at an old warehouse, which could accommodate more people. Reconstruction was completed by 1982, and the church was rededicated on May 3, 1982, exactly 150 years from the date of the original dedication in 1832. The building stands as a tribute to the persistent work of the priest and his parishioners.

Although none of the original santero art remains in the church, for the 150th anniversary celebration the author was commissioned to create an altar screen containing the saints depicted in the nineteenth-century altar screen of the original church. This screen consists of nine panels and a lunette top-piece, each depicting a patron saint from the surrounding missions. The framework for the screen was built by Don Cash, the author's husband, and the screen was installed with the help of many members of the parish. Stations of the cross were also painted by the author and framed in tin by Don Cash.

SAN JUAN NEPOMUCENO
El Rito
FEAST DAY: May 16

SANTA CRUZ
Ojo Caliente
FEAST DAY: May 3

S A N T A   C R U Z

Ojo Caliente

*L*OCATED 1/4 MILE WEST OF U.S. 285, 25 MILES north of Española, Ojo Caliente was settled in the 1730s as a fortress against Indian raids but was abandoned in 1748 because of a Ute attack. After two unsuccessful attempts to reestablish the village in 1766 and 1790, a permanent settlement was established by grant in 1793. The adobe church was not built until around 1820 and was abandoned in 1930. The corrugated metal pitched roof was added in the 1920s, covering up the clerestory window. The buttresses at the front and rear were also added later. The interior has a wood floor and a dirt board ceiling with vigas and corbels. There are niches built into the walls. The old church still contains its original altar railing, and, in 1989, fragments of its nineteenth-century altar screen were discovered embedded in the wood ceiling. In recent years the New Mexico Community Foundation has undertaken restoration and stabilization of this historic church.

A new church was constructed in 1939 and is decorated by a large contemporary altar screen commissioned by one of the local families and painted by the author. It contains six panels and a lunette top-piece, built and assembled by Don Cash, the author's husband, and raised with the assistance of members of the parish.

CHAPTER FIVE

The Taos Area

ALTHOUGH INDIVIDUAL RANCHOS *were established as early as 1617,* Taos, *a predominately Hispanic community, was settled in the 1790s near Taos Pueblo (located 2 miles north of the town), probably the most visited and photographed of all the pueblos. Historically, Taos was the meeting ground for Indians of the Río Grande Valley and nomadic tribes from the mountains and plains, Spanish settlers, beaver trappers, and traders from the Santa Fe Trail. The town is dramatically situated, resting on a high plain like Santa Fe and surrounded by the Sangre de Cristo range and Taos Mountain. Many artists have flocked to Taos, intrigued by its mystical qualities. Among them were J. H. Sharp, Ernest Blumenschein, and Bert Phillips, who together formed the nucleus of the Taos Society of Artists in 1912, and who brought worldwide recognition to Taos as an art center. Later, the famous English writer D. H. Lawrence lived near Taos, brought to New Mexico by the well-known socialite Mabel Dodge Luhan. In addition to the many historic sites, art galleries, and museums in Taos, the spectacular geological formation of the Río Grande Gorge is close by. The Río Grande Gorge Bridge, which hovers 650 feet above the turbulent river at the bottom of the narrow gorge, is located on U.S. 64 about 15 miles northwest of Taos.*

When touring the historic churches, driving from the south, the first village you will arrive at is Pilar, a few miles from Ranchos de Taos. From here on it is necessary to watch for road signs, since some of the villages are only marked with small, sometimes barely visible signs. Careful attention must be paid to maps in order to take advantage of the many churches that can be seen in this area. It will take at least a full day to view the sights of this historic area.

Although many of the smaller missions will undoubtedly be closed, the exterior architecture of these buildings is nevertheless of interest. Several of these missions are only a few minutes drive from the historic Ranchos de Taos Plaza. Taos Pueblo is generally open to the public, but visitors must register at the pueblo offices and pay a minimal fee before proceeding to visit any area. Photographic policies must also be strictly adhered to.

After visiting the churches in Taos and its outskirts, head towards the colorful Arroyo Hondo Valley, where there are two historic churches—at Arroyo Hondo and Arroyo Seco. The smaller village churches at Valdes and San Cristóbal are situated within a 5-mile radius of the Arroyo Seco parish church, only a short distance from the snowcapped peaks of the Taos Ski Valley.

NUESTRA SEÑORA DE LOS DOLORES

Pilar

*L*OCATED 17 MILES SOUTHWEST OF TAOS, THE community of Pilar was settled in 1795 by a grant signed by Fernando Chacón, the governor of New Mexico. The adobe church was not built until 1892, however. It has a red-ribbed metal panel pitched roof with a wood-louvered belfry and gable ends, double-hung windows, and an unusual entry portico. The interior has wood floors and vigas of graduating sizes. There is a date inscribed on the southernmost viga of the interior, probably indicating the year in which it was reroofed.

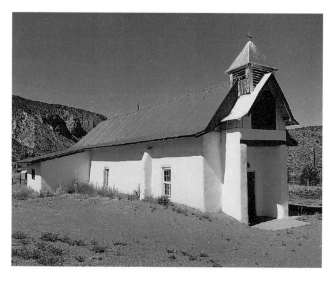

NUESTRA SEÑORA DE LOS DOLORES
Pilar
FEAST DAY: September 15

NUESTRA SEÑORA DE CARMEN

Llano Quemado

*L*OCATED 1/2 MILE SOUTH OF RANCHOS DE TAOS, the village of Llano Quemado, whose name means "burnt plain," first appeared in church records in 1787; however, villagers attended the parish church for over a century before building their own adobe church in the 1940s. The church has a flat roof and wooden belfry; the apse is semicircular, and a concrete apron surrounds the church. The interior has wood floors and a tile ceiling. The altar screen from this church, painted by Rafael Aragón, is now in the Palace of the Governors in Santa Fe on loan from the Spanish Colonial Society, which purchased it many years ago.

NUESTRA SEÑORA DE CARMEN
Llano Quemado
FEAST DAY: July 18

SAN FRANCISCO DE ASÍS

Ranchos de Taos

*T*HE VILLAGE OF RANCHOS DE TAOS, 5 MILES south of Taos, was originally founded as San Francisco de las Trampas. By 1779, settlers had moved from Taos Pueblo, where they had taken refuge from Comanche Indian attacks almost twenty years before. A large enclosed plaza was constructed on the Río de las Trampas, and this became the first community in the valley to be resettled. Because of ongoing Indian raids, it was not until 1803 that a license was granted to build the church for the village, which many historians believe was completed about 1810 (although some historians believe that the church was being built as early as 1776).

Located in the center of the large plaza, the massive adobe church, 120 feet long, has been continuously in use since its construction, although it has undergone several renovations. Originally, it was mud-plastered, but by 1967 the church had been hard-plastered. Then in 1979, the parishioners removed the stucco and replastered the structure with mud; they continue to mud-plaster it periodically, a job that often takes several hundred people about nine days to complete. The church has massive buttresses at the rear of the building. The interior has a high ceiling with vigas, handcarved and painted corbels, and a clerestory window; the original floors were made from local clay, which is still visible in the choir loft. During the past fifty years, the floors were covered with pine boards and then linoleum.

The church contains many examples of early santero work, including the largest altar screen in a New Mexican church; painted by Molleno around 1815, it covers approximately 425 square feet. This side altar screen contains images of Saint Polycarpus (San Policarpio) and Saint Lawrence (San Lorenzo), a tribute to the donors of the screen, Policarpio and Lorenzo Córdova, residents of Ranchos

SAN FRANCISCO DE ASÍS

Ranchos de Taos

FEAST DAY: October 4

de Taos. Two large, carved images flank the altar screen (both excellent examples of the artwork of Molleno), Our Lady of Sorrows (Nuestra Señora de los Dolores) and a Dutch saint, Saint Lydwina (Santa Liduvina). The main altar screen was also built and painted by Molleno at the same time, but the panels were replaced with oil paintings sometime later; the fate of these panels is not known. Both altar screens have undergone extensive restoration in recent years, with the restorers following the faded lines of the originals.

San Francisco de Asís is perhaps the most photographed and painted church in New Mexico. Its image from the rear showing the massive buttresses has appeared in virtually every publication in the Southwest, and it has been painted from many angles and in a variety of styles by many artists, both famous and amateur. The church is surrounded by old adobe buildings, one of which now houses the church gift shop, where a mysterious painting of Christ is displayed. The Ranchos de Taos church is always open to respectful visitors, although there is a strict photographic policy which is enforced.

Once a year during feast day activities, new mayordomos are elected to replace the parishioners who served the previous year. The mayordomos for the parish church and its surrounding missions each receive a retablo of the patron saint painted by the author and framed in tin by Santa Fe tinsmith Don Cash. The Ranchos de Taos church itself usually has six to eight mayordomos who serve annually.

The feast day is celebrated on October 4 with festivities which include a parish fair. A candlelight procession to the church is held the evening before. Other celebrations during the year include a midnight mass on Christmas Eve, preceded by a procession of parishioners carrying pitch-pine torches, and a Comanche Dance performed on New Year's Day in the plaza in front of the church.

NUESTRA SEÑORA DE SAN JUAN DEL RÍO CHIQUITO

Talpa

THE EARLY VILLAGE OF NUESTRA SEÑORA DEL RÍO Chiquito was settled around the beginning of the nineteenth century, but the formal community was not established until 1823 when Manuel Lucero donated a parcel of land to twenty settlers for the purpose of building a plaza. Since there were approximately thirty families living in the village, the need for a chapel arose.

The public chapel of Nuestra Señora de San Juan del Río Chiquito, located several miles southeast of the plaza of Ranchos de Taos on N.M. 518, was built in 1828 and paid for by Bernardo Durán, one of the community's most prosperous citizens. Until 1833, only prayer services and novenas were held in the chapel, and parishioners still traveled to the Ranchos de Taos church for services. Still in use today, it is a small adobe structure with cement-plastered walls, and with an adobe belfry flanked by two short towers; the interior has wood floors and a tile ceiling.

The small, ornate altar screen in the chapel was painted by the santero Molleno in 1828 and is dedicated to Our Lady of Talpa (Nuestra Señora de Talpa), its patron saint. Among the saints depicted in the panels is Saint Bernard (San Bernardino), the patron saint of the donor, Bernardo Durán. Santeros often paid tribute to benefactors by including their patron saint in the altar screens. The patron saint of the community, Our Lady of Saint John of the Lakes (Nuestra Señora de San Juan de los Lagos), is interchangeable with Our Lady of Talpa. The image of Our Lady of Saint John of the Lakes, which is housed in the central niche of the altar screen, was carved by Rafael Aragón. Her extensive wardrobe consists of satin gowns, capes, jewels, and crowns changed regularly by the mayordomos.

The feast day is celebrated on October 7, which is also the feast day of Our Lady of the Rosary. Feast day events include vespers, a procession, and a mass, followed by food and other festivities.

NUESTRA SEÑORA DE SAN JUAN DEL RÍO CHIQUITO

Talpa

FEAST DAY: October 7

CONCEPCIÓN INMACULADA

Ranchitos

*T*HE VILLAGE IS A SETTLEMENT ALONG TAOS Canyon, 2 miles west of Taos. Its name means "little ranches," which indicates a smaller settlement than those signified by the term "ranchos." The village was settled by families who wished to grow their crops in a smaller locality than Taos, but still be in the protective area of the larger town. The small adobe church was built in 1867. It has a wood-shingled pitched roof and a wooden belfry, and the windows are hand-constructed in a neo-Gothic style. The feast day is celebrated with a mass and a procession.

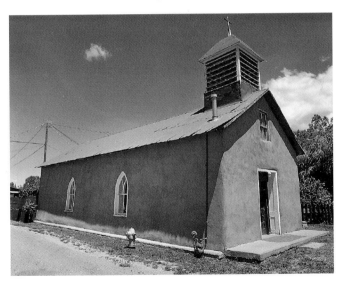

CONCEPCIÓN INMACULADA
Ranchitos
FEAST DAY: December 8

SAN ANTONIO DE PADUA

La Loma

*L*A LOMA IS A SMALL VILLAGE ON THE WESTERN outskirts of Taos. Said to be the Jeantet family chapel, the adobe church was built in 1892. Jean Jeantet was a Canadian fur trapper who married a Taos native in 1829. His son, Gabriel, was known as a master carpenter who set up a wheel lathe in his Taos workshop and began producing remarkable turned pieces in a new style, including a large niche for the patron saint of this chapel, Saint Anthony of Padua (San Antonio de Padua). The church has a corrugated metal pitched roof with a wooden belfry and gable ends. Flagstone veneer has been added to the front of the church in recent years.

SAN ANTONIO DE PADUA
La Loma
FEAST DAY: June 16

SAN GERÓNIMO DE TAOS

Taos Pueblo

*T*AOS PUEBLO IS LOCATED APPROXIMATELY 75 miles north of Santa Fe, 3 miles northeast of Taos, at the foothills of the Sangre de Cristo Mountains. Construction of the fortress-like church on the western outskirts of the pueblo was begun in 1706; its adobe walls are over 31 inches thick. In January of 1847, during the Taos Uprising, the church was used as a sanctuary by the rebelling pueblos. (It was during this uprising that Charles Bent, the governor of New Mexico, was scalped and killed.) In this confrontation, the pueblo church was almost completely destroyed by United States government troops, and the ruins of it are still visible.

The new church was built around 1850 at a nearby site and remodeled in 1920 when a wooden belfry was added. It is of adobe construction and has double bell towers; the interior has wood floors, and its ceiling is comprised of vigas and corbels. The church is the center of pueblo life; its plastered exterior white walls compete with the sun for brilliance during warm summer days. A stream from the Río del Pueblo, which rises at the pueblo's sacred Blue Lake, flows nearby, beckoning the pueblo children.

There are several examples of eighteenth- and nineteenth-century santero art in this church, all well preserved and cared for by the *fiscales* (pueblo church officials) assigned these duties. Santos, dressed in colors that reflect the seasons of the year, sit in niches of various sizes on the walls surrounding the altar table. In addition, there is a large eighteenth-century Christ in the Tomb (El Santo Entierro) which remains completely covered until Holy Week services at Easter time.

The feast day is celebrated on September 30. On the eve of September 29, vespers and dances are held. On the feast day itself, there is a trade fair, as well as pole climbing and ceremonial races and dances. There are many other celebrations at Taos Pueblo throughout the year. A Green Corn Dance is held on May 3, Santa Cruz Day. A Corn Dance is also performed on June 13, the feast day of Saint Anthony of Padua (San Antonio de Padua), and on July 25, the feast of Saint James (Santiago) and Saint Anne (Santa Ana). On December 24, there is a sundown torchlight procession at the pueblo in honor of the Virgin, followed on Christmas Day by a Matachines or a Deer Dance.

SAN GERÓNIMO DE TAOS
Taos Pueblo
FEAST DAY: September 30

SANTÍSIMA TRINIDAD

Arroyo Seco

*T*HIS IS THE PARISH CHURCH FOR THE AREA, located a few miles east of Arroyo Hondo off N.M. 150. It is comprised of two churches—a church built in the early 1800s and a newer church built in the 1980s. The 1800s church is of thick-walled adobe construction with a corrugated metal pitched roof and a wooden belfry. It has double-hung windows and a wood gable above the entry door. The interior has wood floors, vigas, and corbels. For many years the building has been used as a weaving cooperative by local weavers.

Because of its historic significance, the New Mexico Community Foundation has recently undertaken restoration and stabilization of this structure. The older church contains a large altar screen painted by the santero José de Gracia Gonzales around 1860. The new church contains a magnificent Cristo carved by Rafael Aragón, which is now permanently attached to the altar, and a unique carving of the Holy Trinity (Santísima Trinidad) by the Arroyo Hondo Santero, set into the side altar; both pieces were transferred from the old church.

The mayordomos who serve this parish and the surrounding mission churches are elected before each feast day. For the services they have rendered in the past year, each mayordomo is given a gift by the priest which consists of a retablo of the patron saint painted by the author and framed in tin by Santa Fe tinsmith Don Cash. The parish has at least twenty mayordomos who serve annually.

The feast day is celebrated with vespers the evening before; on the feast day itself there is a mass, followed by a procession through town or around the chapel, a ceremony exchanging mayordomos, and other festivities.

SANTÍSIMA TRINIDAD
Arroyo Seco
FEAST DAY: September 15

NUESTRA SEÑORA DE LOS DOLORES

Arroyo Hondo

*I*N 1830, SIMEON TURLEY ESTABLISHED HIS RANCH near this Spanish settlement 12 miles northwest of Taos, named for the deep valley in which it is situated. He installed a waterwheel and built a mill to grind grain, resulting in a distillery which became known all over the frontier. (Turley was later killed in an Indian uprising in 1847.) As the village grew, it became one of the first outposts along the mountains traveling from Taos north into Colorado.

The church was built in the early 1830s and is of adobe construction, mud-plastered as needed by the parishioners; it survived almost a century before extensive remodeling was undertaken. In 1916, Father Joseph Giraud, a French priest who intensely disliked the architecture of the area, had the massive corner buttresses removed and a pitched shingle roof added, along with a wood-shingled belfry. The windows were torn out and replaced by neo-Gothic style windows; and a modern school bell was installed instead of the old Spanish bell. The church now resembled a New England Victorian Gothic chapel rather than the quaint adobe church it once was.

In honor of the 150th anniversary of the church in 1983, the parish priest and the parishioners removed the tile ceiling, which had been added during the 1916 remodeling, exposing the original vigas. The priest also commissioned the author and her husband to reproduce a fifteen-panel altar screen based on the original screen painted in 1830 by a santero known as the Arroyo Hondo Painter, which was removed from the church and eventually sold to the Taylor Museum in Colorado Springs, Colorado, in the 1900s. Although only a few pieces of the santero art that was originally in the church remain there today, the original artwork of this church

NUESTRA SEÑORA DE LOS DOLORES
Arroyo Hondo
FEAST DAY: September 15

is highlighted in a book published by the Taylor Museum/Colorado Springs Fine Arts Center entitled, *Arroyo Hondo*. The feast day is celebrated with a mass, a procession, and a parish fiesta.

SAN CRISTÓBAL

San Cristóbal

*L*OCATED NORTH OF ARROYO HONDO, THE ADOBE church in this small farming community was not built until 1945, even though the village had been settled since 1860. It has a shingled pitched roof, concrete belfry, and aluminum double-hung windows.

There is a local legend about the naming of the church which is as follows: a group of men from Quemado were digging near the church, accompanied by an *Americano* who was paying them to dig. After digging several deep holes, they rested until the next day, when they began again early in the morning. That day while digging they encountered a deep pit walled with cedar poles. In it were several objects, the largest very heavy, all wrapped in buckskin and tied with leather. As one of the villagers picked up the heaviest object, the buckskin became loose, and the object fell back into the pit. It was a large golden image of Saint Christopher (San Cristóbal). After they removed everything from the pit, the men were paid and sent away. It is not known what happened to the golden image, but the church was named San Cristóbal because of it. Several miles from the village is the site of the D. H. Lawrence Ranch, now owned by the University of New Mexico.

SAN CRISTÓBAL
San Cristóbal
FEAST DAY: last week of July

SAN ANTONIO DE PADUA
Questa
FEAST DAY: June 16

SAN ANTONIO DE PADUA

Questa

*T*HE VILLAGE OF QUESTA, LOCATED 22 MILES north of Taos, was settled in 1835 as San Antonio del Río Colorado, but soon thereafter the villagers were dispersed by bands of raiding Indians. They resettled permanently in 1842 after using the area temporarily for several years to grow crops during the summer months. The name of the village was changed to Questa in 1884 when the post office was established.

The adobe church was built around the 1860s. It is in the cruciform style with two side chapels. It has a pitched metal roof painted red, and double towers with louvered windows and a portal in the center. The interior has wood floors, vigas with large corbels, and a contemporary altar screen of local origin.

NUESTRA SEÑORA DE GUADALUPE

Cerro

*L*OCATED 3 MILES NORTHWEST OF QUESTA, THE village was settled in 1854 and is named for the Cerro Guadalupe Mountains which run adjacent to it. The adobe church was not built until 1940, since parishioners could easily travel to Questa for services. It has a pitched shingle roof with double towers. The bell is housed above the parapet. The interior has fixed glass windows, wood floors, and a tile ceiling.

NUESTRA SEÑORA DE GUADALUPE
Cerro
FEAST DAY: December 12

CHAPTER SIX

The Mora Area

THE MORA VALLEY, *at the foothills of the Rincon Mountains northwest of Las Vegas, was settled by Spaniards around 1818. Some years later, after the Santa Fe Trail opened, this beautiful mountainous area was heavily populated by French traders, as reflected by various village names, such as Ledoux and Gascon. Today, the area consists of many small farming communities situated close to the Mora River.*

The valley is accessible via either the highway to Las Vegas or the highway to Taos. If time is a factor, the drive through Las Vegas is faster, but the drive through Taos offers magnificent alpine scenery and possibilities for numerous cultural side trips. Once at Mora, the visitor must determine which missions are to be visited and in which order, since there are many diverse historic churches and no circuitous route one can follow from church to church. In addition, it is wise to check area maps to determine whether a four-wheel drive vehicle might be required to reach the more remote churches.

SANTA GERTRUDES

Mora

THE VILLAGE OF MORA WAS FOUNDED BY A LARGE land grant from Governor Albino Perez to José Tapia and seventy-five other grantees in 1835, although the village was probably occupied before that time. Tapia was later killed by Indians. Ceran St. Vrain, a Frenchman of many occupations—trapper, soldier, and merchant—moved to Mora from Taos in 1885 and established several sawmills, which provided lumber for nearby Fort Union as well as jobs for the local villagers. He also established a distillery and a gristmill, a large two-story stone mill with a gambrel roof that still survives today. After his death he was honored with the largest funeral ever held in the area, including a mass at the adobe church.

Built in 1835, Santa Gertrudes is said to be the first church erected in the area. It has a recessed porch with a wooden gable above it. In 1972, a modern church was built nearby, and the old church is now used as a parish hall.

SANTA GERTRUDES
Mora
FEAST DAY: November 16

S A N   I S I D R O

Holman

*L*OCATED 5 MILES NORTHWEST OF MORA, THE ADOBE church in this small community was not built until the 1950s, even though the town had been in existence since the late 1800s. The church has a wood-shingled pitched roof and belfry, and is surrounded by a stone wall. In July of 1975, an image of Christ was believed by many to have appeared on the wall of the old schoolhouse in Holman, attracting nationwide attention and thousands of visitors who viewed it as a miracle. The feast day is celebrated with vespers, a mass, and a procession, during which the patron saint is carried to nearby fields so that the crops may be blessed.

SAN ISIDRO
Holman
FEAST DAY: May 15

CAPILLA DE SAN ANTONIO

Servilleta/Chacón

*C*APILLA DE SAN ANTONIO IS LOCATED 21 MILES northwest of Taos on U.S. 285 in a small farming community near Mora. The town was named for members of the prominent Chacón family, who were among the valley's original settlers in the middle 1860s. The adobe chapel was built in 1865 and at one time had as its patron saint Saint Isidore the Farmer (San Isidro Labrador). The chapel is in the cruciform style and has a cement-stucco exterior. The interior has wood floors and a curved ceiling, with gypsum-plastered walls. There is a graveyard next to the church. The feast day is celebrated with a mass and a procession, followed by a fiesta.

CAPILLA DE SAN ANTONIO
Servilleta/Chacón
FEAST DAY: June 16

S A N T O   N I Ñ O

Monte Aplanado

*L*OCATED 1/2 MILE FROM THIS VILLAGE IN THE
Mora area, the adobe church was built in the 1830s, in conjunction
with the Mora land grant. It has a corrugated metal pitched roof
and wooden belfry, which was added in 1918. There is a buttress
on the southwest corner. The interior has a concrete floor covered
with linoleum, panel walls, and a wood ceiling covering the original
church. A graveyard surrounds the church. The feast day is celebrated
on a date chosen by the priest and parishioners with vespers, a
mass, and a procession, during which the fields are blessed.

SANTO NIÑO
Monte Aplanado
FEAST DAY: date varies

S A N   J O S E

Ledoux

*L*OCATED WEST OF N.M. 94 IN THE MORA AREA, THE village was named for an early French fur trapper and established in the late 1800s to accommodate the influx of settlers coming to the area. Parishioners attended mass at the parish church in Mora until 1906, when the community had grown large enough to support its own church. The structure is of adobe and has a corrugated metal pitched roof and wooden belfry, with a cement-stucco interior. It has wood-shingled gables and stained-glass windows. The interior has wood floors and a nave with a small barrel vault ceiling supported by columns.

SAN JOSÉ
Ledoux
FEAST DAY: March 19

NUESTRA SEÑORA DE CARMEN

El Carmen

*L*OCATED 12 MILES SOUTH OF MORA, THE VILLAGE is situated near the Cebolla River and is one of the many small farming towns located in the Mora Valley. Built in 1900, the church is named for its patron saint, Our Lady of Mount Carmel. It has a cement-stucco exterior and a pitched roof and belfry, which was added later. The interior has wood floors and vigas. The graveyard and ruins of a nineteenth-century church are in the churchyard.

NUESTRA SEÑORA DE CARMEN
El Carmen
FEAST DAY: July 18

S A N   I S I D R O

Sapello

*L*OCATED 13 MILES NORTH OF LAS VEGAS, THE village is situated in the foothills of the mountains at the confluence of the Sapello and Manuelito creeks at the turnoff leading to N.M. 94. This small farming community bears one of New Mexico's oldest names, which may be derived from the word *sepillo*, meaning hairbrush. Near the village is a Santa Fe Trail landmark, Hermit's Peak, a large granite outcropping. This was the former home of a reclusive holy man, Giovanni Marie Augustini, who reputedly gave up all his worldly possessions to live on this mesa top in the 1860s—hence the name "Hermit's Peak."

The adobe church, no longer in use, was probably built in the mid-1800s. It was replaced in the 1940s by Nuestra Señora de Guadalupe, a more modern church. The older church has a pitched corrugated metal roof with a wooden belfry and metal gable ends.

The feast day is celebrated with a blessing of the fields by the patron saint, Saint Isidore the Farmer (San Isidro Labrador).

SAN ISIDRO
Sapello
FEAST DAY: May 15

SAN ACACIO DE LAS GOLONDRINAS

Golondrinas

*L*OCATED 5 MILES EAST OF N.M. 518 ON N.M. 161, THE adobe church was built in 1862. It has 32-inch adobe walls with mud-plaster on the nave and cement-plaster on the east facade. Its roof is of corrugated steel, and it has a wooden belfry and shingled gable ends. The entry door is raised panel with a rounded transom. The interior has wood floors and vigas, with all the necessary illumination being provided by candlelight. The community is named for the profusion of swallows which inhabit the area.

SAN ACACIO DE LAS GOLONDRINAS
Golondrinas
FEAST DAY: June 22

SANTO NIÑO DE ATOCHA

Buena Vista

*B*UENA VISTA, WHICH MEANS "PRETTY VIEW," IS located 20 miles north of Las Vegas and 1 1/2 miles south of La Cueva in the Mora area. The adobe church was built in 1876. The walls are 30 inches thick, plastered with cement. It has a corrugated metal pitched roof with a wooden belfry and wood-shingled gables. The interior has wood floors, and the walls are of painted gypsum plaster. The feast day is celebrated on a date chosen by the priest and parishioners; during the festivities the patron saint is carried around to each farm as the fields are blessed.

SANTO NIÑO DE ATOCHA
Buena Vista
FEAST DAY: date varies

S A N   R A F A E L

La Cueva

*L*OCATED AT THE JUNCTION OF N.M. 518/442, NORTH of the mill near Salman Ranch, the village of La Cueva was established in 1851 by Vicente Romero after the construction of Fort Union. It is a National Historic District belonging to the Salman family. The now abandoned adobe church was built in 1862, and recently the New Mexico Community Foundation and local villagers have made efforts to restore it. It is of 28-inch-thick mud-plastered walls and has a wood-shingled pitched roof, belfry, and gable rafters. The windows and door are in a French Gothic style. The interior has mud-plastered walls painted with gesso and flat paint, pine floors, and a painted wood ceiling of tongue-and-groove construction.

SAN RAFAEL
La Cueva
FEAST DAY: October 24

SAGRADO CORAZÓN

Rainsville

*L*OCATED 8 MILES EAST OF MORA, OFF N.M. 442, this village was formerly known as Coyote. The village was established because the Mora area had grown to the extent that many farmers felt they needed additional acreage to grow their crops, which helped feed soldiers at nearby Fort Union.

The adobe church was built in 1910. It is in the cruciform style and has 26-inch walls, a corrugated metal pitched roof, a wood-shingled belfry, and neo-Gothic windows. The interior has wood floors covered with linoleum, a painted battened ceiling, and an organ loft above the entry. A graveyard surrounds the church.

SAGRADO CORAZÓN
Rainsville
FEAST DAY: May 3

S A N T A R I T A

Lucero

*L*OCATED IN THE CENTER OF THE VILLAGE OF Lucero (formerly Plaza Coyote) on a dirt road west of N.M. 442, 7 miles northeast of Mora, the village was established by the descendants of Pedro Lucero de Godoy, a native of Mexico City who came to northern New Mexico in the early seventeenth century. His sons and grandsons were prominent participants in the reconquest of New Mexico, which took place in 1692. The adobe church was built in 1886, shortly after the post office was established in the community. It has a corrugated metal pitched roof, a wooden belfry, and double-hung windows. The exterior is mud-plastered. The interior has wood floors and a pressed board ceiling.

SANTA RITA
Lucero
FEAST DAY: May 22

SANTA TERESA DEL NIÑO JESÚS

El Turquillo

*L*OCATED ON N.M. 434, 7 MILES NORTH OF THE junction with N.M. 518 in the Mora area, the adobe church was built in 1920, shortly after the post office was established in the village. It has a corrugated metal pitched roof with a wooden bell tower. The interior has a concrete floor and plastered gypsum board ceilings; it has undergone recent remodelings. A graveyard surrounds the church.

SANTA TERESA DEL NIÑO JESÚS
El Turquillo
FEAST DAY: October 15

S A N   I S I D R O

Ojo Feliz

*L*OCATED 1/4 MILE EAST OF N.M. 442 AT THE BOTTOM of a hill in the north end of this village in the Mora area, the adobe church was built in 1900. It has a pitched metal corrugated roof and wooden belfry, which was added later. The interior has wood floors and a square-beamed ceiling. The feast day is celebrated with vespers, a mass, and a procession around the nearby fields for the blessing of the crops.

SAN ISIDRO
Ojo Feliz
FEAST DAY: May 15

NUESTRA SEÑORA DE GUADALUPE

Ocate

*L*OCATED 1/4 MILE NORTH OF THE INTERSECTION of N.M. 120 and N.M. 442, 24 miles northwest of Wagon Mound near Mora, the adobe church in this small farming community was built in 1900, although the area had been settled many years before. The church has been extensively remodeled in recent years. It is in the cruciform plan with a corrugated pitched metal roof and a wooden belfry built on a second tier. The interior has wood floors and vaulted ceilings.

NUESTRA SEÑORA DE GUADALUPE
Ocate
FEAST DAY: December 12

CHAPTER SEVEN

The Pecos Area

ALTHOUGH THE PECOS AREA, *located on N.M. 63, just north of I-25, 20 miles east of Santa Fe is not considered part of northern New Mexico per se, it is included here because of the architectural similarity between churches around Pecos and the village churches of the north and because of the historical significance of the churches. Moreover, the churches at such villages as Cañoncito and Rowe reflect the same warmth and community involvement as the churches in the north. The dominant geographical feature of the area is the Pecos River, which flows serenely down the mountains near the town for which it was named. It irrigates thousands of acres of farmlands and also provides recreation and waterfowl areas. The Pecos National Monument continues to preserve the ruins of a centuries-old mission church and a pueblo which was one of the most important sites at the time the Spaniards entered New Mexico.*

After visiting the churches close to I-25, turn onto N.M. 3 toward Villanueva. Here lush green valleys alongside the river provide a tranquil backdrop for the three churches at Ribera, Sena, and Villanueva. The historic San Miguel del Vado was the port of entry for New Mexico on the Santa Fe Trail, and traveling merchants were required to have the goods which they were bringing into the province checked. Upon reaching the top of the hill at Villanueva, it is necessary to retrace the route back to the main highway, passing Villanueva State Park nearby. The many old adobe houses along this route, with their pitched corrugated tin roofs, picket fences, and lace-curtained windows—some still inhabited, some abandoned— add to the ambience of a bygone era.

NUESTRA SEÑORA DE LA LUZ

Cañoncito

*T*HIS CHURCH IS LOCATED ON THE I-25 FRONTAGE road at Cañoncito (Apache Canyon Exit), 15 miles southeast of Santa Fe. The village has a long and interesting history, dating from the Civil War, during which several important battles were fought near this site. Cañoncito was the last station on the Santa Fe Trail before entering Santa Fe. The adobe church was built in the late 1800s. It is of adobe construction with a recently replaced metal pitched roof and wooden belfry. There is a stone buttress in front. A colorful graveyard surrounds the church.

NUESTRA SEÑORA DE LA LUZ
Cañoncito
FEAST DAY: May 21

SAGRADA FAMILIA

Rowe

*L*OCATED OFF I-25 AT U.S. 84/85 FRONTAGE ROAD, the village was named in 1876 for a contractor on the Santa Fe Railroad. It is noted for the high mesa which looms over the area. The adobe church was built in 1894, eighteen years after the village was established. It is in the cruciform style and has a pitched metal roof with a louvered wooden belfry and spire added later. The interior has wood floors and a wood ceiling. The graveyard is to the rear of the church.

SAGRADA FAMILIA
Rowe
FEAST DAY: first Sunday after January 6

SAN MIGUEL DEL VADO

Ribera

*I*N 1794, FIFTY-ONE SETTLERS CAMPED ON THE BANKS of the Pecos River as they made adobe bricks to build their village. Originally established as an outpost against raiding Indians, this village has a long and fascinating history involving merchants traveling over the Santa Fe Trail. It is located 2 miles south of I-25 on N.M. 3, about 35 miles southeast of Santa Fe.

The fortress-like adobe church was built in the early 1800s in the cruciform style on a man-made elevation surrounded by a low wall. The corrugated metal pitched roof and two towers with louvered windows were added after 1850. It has a round attic window with petal-shaped glass. The interior walls are gesso over mud-plaster, and the wood ceiling covers vigas and corbels. There is a graveyard in the churchyard. The bell in the tower is inscribed with the date 1830, and the bell in the yard with the date 1861.

SAN MIGUEL DEL VADO
Ribera
FEAST DAY: September 29

S A N   I S I D R O

Gonzales Ranch

*L*OCATED OFF COUNTY ROAD B30A&B IN SAN Miguel County, 4 miles south of Rowe on the road to Villanueva, the village was homesteaded in 1920 by Juan Cristóbal Gonzales and four of his brothers. One of these brothers was José Antonio Gonzales, who came from Lovato, a small settlement near Sena. Cristóbal Gonzales, grandson of Juan Cristóbal, still lives in the village.

The church was built in 1932 by Cristóbal's father, Tomás Gonzales, Pablo Sena, Beatrice Gonzales, and Juan de Díos Gonzales. It is constructed of stone and has a corrugated metal pitched roof. The interior has a wood floor and ceiling. There is a graveyard in the churchyard. Mass is held twice a month; and the feast day of the patron saint, Saint Isidore the Farmer (San Isidro Labrador), is celebrated on May 15, with vespers, a mass, and a procession for the blessing of the fields. The feast of a second patron saint, Saint Theresa (Santa Teresa), is celebrated on October 15.

SAN ISIDRO

Gonzales Ranch

FEAST DAYS: May 15 and October 15

NUESTRO SEÑOR DE ESQUÍPULAS

Sena

LOCATED 8 MILES SOUTH OF I-25 ON N.M. 3, THE village was named for the Bernardino de Sena family, who came to New Mexico in 1693 following De Vargas's reconquest. He remained in Santa Fe, and some of his descendants populated the area. In Santa Fe, historic Sena Plaza remains as a monument to his name.

The adobe church was built in 1908, seven years after the establishment of the post office in the village. It has 32-inch walls, a corrugated metal pitched roof, and a wooden belfry. The interior has wood floors and a wood ceiling covered by painted pressboard. There is a graveyard in the churchyard.

NUESTRO SEÑOR DE ESQUÍPULAS
Sena
FEAST DAY: January 15

NUESTRA SEÑORA DE GUADALUPE

Villanueva

LOCATED ON N.M. 3, ABOUT 11 MILES SOUTH OF I-25, the village of Villanueva (which means "new town") was not settled by a land grant but rather by people who came here from various areas of New Mexico in the late eighteenth century. Because of the threat of raiding Indians, the settlers only stayed in the village during the spring, summer, and fall months, always leaving after the harvest of their chile and other vegetable crops. After 1825, when the threat of Indian raids decreased, the villagers were willing to attempt living there full time, and they began to build their adobe houses with shining peaked tin roofs on the road that twists and winds along the bluffs above the Pecos River.

The adobe-stone church was built between 1818 and 1826. It is in the cruciform style and has exterior cement-plastered walls, a pitched corrugated metal roof, and a wooden belfry. The interior has painted plaster walls with a viga and corbel ceiling. Surrounding the church is a 3-foot stone wall. A convent was added when the Sisters of the Sorrowful Mother came to teach, and a rectory is attached to the side of the church. The stone veneer was added to the front of the church in the 1940s. In 1986, the church was partially destroyed by a fire.

The women of the village have embroidered a tapestry which circles the interior walls of the church, each section depicting a period in the long history of the community. Well-known Santa Fe painter Federico Vigil executed a fresco for the church which was dedicated on the Feast of Corpus Christi.

NUESTRA SEÑORA DE GUADALUPE
Villanueva
FEAST DAY: December 12

APPENDIX
The Churches of Northern New Mexico
and Their Construction Dates

Because the Archdiocese of Santa Fe did not have a complete list of construction dates for the northern churches, a list was compiled using every historical source available. Where two or more sources indicated the same construction date, that date was used; where there was only one date available, that date was used with a plus or minus symbol following it. An asterisk (*) indicates those churches that are discussed and illustrated in this book.

THE SANTA FE AREA

*Cristo Rey (Christ the King), Santa Fe, 1939
*Loretto Chapel (Our Lady of Light), Santa Fe, 1878–
*Nuestra Señora de Guadalupe (Our Lady of Guadalupe), Cañada de los Alamos, 1922
*Rosario Chapel (Our Lady of the Conquest), Santa Fe, 1807
*Saint Francis Cathedral (San Francisco de Asís) [Parish], Santa Fe, 1714+
*San Diego de Tesuque (Saint Didacus of Tesuque), Tesuque Pueblo, 1877
*San Isidro (Saint Isidore), Agua Fria Village, 1835
*San Miguel (Saint Michael), Santa Fe, 1710+
*Santuario de Guadalupe (Our Lady of Guadalupe), Santa Fe, 1800+–

THE POJOAQUE AREA

Nuestra Señora de Guadalupe (Our Lady of Guadalupe) [Parish], Pojoaque, 1966
*Sagrado Corazón (Sacred Heart), Nambé, 1947
*San Antonio de Padua (Saint Anthony of Padua), El Rancho, 1938
*San Francisco de Asís (Saint Francis of Assisi), Nambé Pueblo, 1974

THE ESPAÑOLA AREA

Nuestra Señora de Guadalupe (Our Lady of Guadalupe), Guachupangue, early 1800s
Sagrado Corazón (Sacred Heart) [Parish], Española, 1947
San Antonio de Padua (Saint Anthony of Padua), El Guache, 1900
*San Francisco de Asís (Saint Francis of Assisi), El Duende, 1896
*San Ildefonso (Saint Ildephonsus), San Ildefonso Pueblo, 1968
*San José de Chama (Saint Joseph of Chama), Hernández, 1850
*Santa Clara (Saint Clare), Santa Clara Pueblo, 1918

THE SAN JUAN PUEBLO AREA

Nuestra Señora de la Soledad (Our Lady of Solitude), La Villita, 1913
San Antonio de Padua (Saint Anthony of Padua), Alcalde, 1878; rebuilt 1954
*San Francisco de Asís (Saint Francis of Assisi), Estaca, 1930+
*San José/San Rafael (Saint Joseph/Saint Raphael), El Guique, 1900+
*San Juan Caballero (Saint John) [Parish], San Juan Pueblo, 1913
*San Pedro (Saint Peter), Chamita, 1875

THE SANTA CRUZ AREA

*La Capilla del Nacimiento del Niño Jesús (Chapel of the Nativity), La Puebla, 1876
*Iglesia de Santa Cruz de la Cañada (Holy Cross of La Cañada) [Parish], Santa Cruz, 1743
*San Isidro (Saint Isidore), La Mesilla, 1918
San Pedro (Saint Peter), San Pedro, 1939
*Sangre de Cristo (Blood of Christ), Cuarteles, 1849
Santo Niño (Holy Child), Santo Niño, 1875

THE CHIMAYÓ AREA

*Nuestra Señora del Rosario (Our Lady of the Rosary), Truchas, 1800+
*San Antonio de Padua (Saint Anthony of Padua), Córdova, early 1830s

*San José de Gracia de las Trampas (Saint Joseph), Las Trampas, 1760

San Miguel del Valle (Saint Michael), El Valle, 1850; rebuilt 1987

Santa Familia (Holy Family) [Parish], Chimayó, 1969

*Santo Domingo (Saint Dominic), Cundiyó, 1838

*Santo Tomás (Saint Thomas), Ojo Sarco, 1886

*Santuario de Chimayó (Sanctuary of Chimayó), Chimayó, 1814

THE PEÑASCO AREA

Concepción Inmaculada (Immaculate Conception), Placitas, 1870+

Nuestra Señora de la Soledad (Our Lady of Solitude), Vadito, 1961

*Sagrado Corazón (Sacred Heart), Río Lucío, 1920

*San Acacio (Saint Acacius), Llano Largo, 1936

San Antonio de Padua (Saint Anthony of Padua) [Parish], Peñasco, 1962

*San Juan Nepomuceno (Saint John Nepomuk), Llano San Juan, 1832+

*San Lorenzo de Picurís (Saint Lawrence of Picurís), Picurís Pueblo, 1776+; rebuilt 1988

Santa Bárbara (Saint Barbara), Rodarte, 1922

Santa Cruz (Holy Cross), Chamisal, 1948

THE ABIQUIÚ AREA

*Christ in the Desert Monastery, Abiquiú, 1964

*Nuestra Señora de Guadalupe (Our Lady of Guadalupe), Gallina, 1954+

San Antonio de Padua (Saint Anthony of Padua), Medanales, 1950

San Juan Bautista (Saint John the Baptist), Coyote, 1867

*San Miguel (Saint Michael), Cañones, 1859

San Pedro (Saint Peter), Youngsville, 1930s

Santa Teresa (Saint Theresa), Mesa de Poleo, 1946+

*Santo Niño (Holy Child), Capulín, 1920+

*Santo Tomás (Saint Thomas), 1773; Santa Rosa de Lima (Saint Rose of Lima) [Parish], Abiquiú, 1744

THE TIERRA AMARILLA AREA

*San José (Saint Joseph), Los Ojos, 1883; rebuilt 1950
*San Juan Nepomuceno (Saint John Nepomuk), Canjilón, 1878
*San Miguel (Saint Michael), La Puente, 1914
 Santo Niño (Holy Child), Cebolla, 1949
*Santo Niño (Holy Child) [Parish], Tierra Amarilla, 1907

THE EL RITO AREA

*Concepción Inmaculada (Immaculate Conception), Tres Piedras, 1990
 Divina Pastora (Divine Shepherdess), Petaca, 1950
*Nuestra Señora de los Dolores (Our Lady of Sorrows), Vallecitos, 1880
*Nuestra Señora de Guadalupe (Our Lady of Guadalupe), La Madera, 1918
 San Antonio de Padua (Saint Anthony of Padua), Placitas, 1920
 San Antonio de Padua (Saint Anthony of Padua), Servilleta, 1880+
*San Juan Nepomuceno (Saint John Nepomuk) [Parish], El Rito, 1832
*San Luis Gonzalo de Amarante (Saint Amarant), Las Tablas, 1899
*Santa Cruz (Holy Cross), Ojo Caliente, 1820+–
 Santa María (Saint Mary), Ojo Caliente, 1939

THE DIXON AREA

*Nuestra Señora de los Dolores (Our Lady of Sorrows), Pilar, 1892
*Nuestra Señora de Guadalupe (Our Lady of Guadalupe), Velarde, 1817
 San Antonio de Padua (Saint Anthony of Padua) [Parish], Dixon, 1929
 San José (Saint Joseph), Lyden, 1897
 Santa Ana (Saint Anne), Embudo, 1810+

THE RANCHOS DE TAOS AREA

*Nuestra Señora de Carmen (Our Lady of Mount Carmel), Llano Quemado, 1940s

Nuestra Señora de San Juan de los Lagos (Our Lady of Saint John of the Lakes), Talpa, 1851

*Nuestra Señora de San Juan del Río Chiquito (Our Lady of Saint John of Río Chiquito), Talpa, 1828

*San Francisco de Asís (Saint Francis of Assisi) [Parish], Ranchos de Taos, 1810+−

San Isidro (Saint Isidore), Los Córdovas, 1832

THE TAOS AREA

*Concepción Inmaculada (Immaculate Conception), Ranchitos, 1867

Nuestra Señora de los Dolores (Our Lady of Sorrows), Cañón, 1900

Nuestra Señora de los Dolores (Our Lady of Sorrows), El Prado, 1900+

Nuestra Señora de Guadalupe (Our Lady of Guadalupe) [Parish], Taos, 1911

*San Antonio de Padua (Saint Anthony of Padua), La Loma, 1892

*San Gerónimo de Taos (Saint Jerome of Taos), Taos Pueblo, 1850

San Miguel (Saint Michael), Ranchitos, 1942

THE ARROYO HONDO AREA

*Nuestra Señora de los Dolores (Our Lady of Sorrows), Arroyo Hondo, early 1830s

San Antonio de Padua (Saint Anthony of Padua), Valdez, mid-1900s

*San Cristóbal (Saint Christopher), San Cristóbal, 1945

*Santísima Trinidad (Holy Trinity) [Parish], Arroyo Seco, 1825+

Santo Niño (Holy Child), Las Colonias, 1930+

THE QUESTA AREA

*Nuestra Señora de Guadalupe (Our Lady of Guadalupe), Cerro, 1940+
Our Lady of the Woods, Red River, 1954+
Sagrado Corazón (Sacred Heart), Costilla, 1890+
*San Antonio de Padua (Saint Anthony of Padua) [Parish], Questa, 1860+
Santo Niño (Holy Child), Amalia, 1914–

THE MORA AREA

*Capilla de San Antonio (Chapel of Saint Anthony), Servilleta/ Chacón, 1865
*Nuestra Señora de Carmen (Our Lady of Mount Carmel), El Carmen, 1900
Nuestra Señora de Guadalupe (Our Lady of Guadalupe), Guadalupita, 1957
*Nuestra Señora de Guadalupe (Our Lady of Guadalupe), Ocate, 1900
*Sagrado Corazón (Sacred Heart), Rainsville, 1910
*San Acacio de las Golondrinas (Saint Acacius of Golondrinas), Golondrinas, 1862
San Antonio de Padua (Saint Anthony of Padua), Cleveland, 1980s
*San José (Saint Joseph), Ledoux, 1906
*San Isidro (Saint Isidore), Holman, 1950s
*San Isidro (Saint Isidore), Ojo Feliz, 1900
*San Isidro (Saint Isidore), Sapello, mid-1800s
*San Rafael (Saint Raphael), La Cueva, 1862
*Santa Gertrudes (Saint Gertrude) [Parish], Mora, 1835
*Santa Rita (Saint Rita), Lucero, 1886
*Santa Teresa del Niño Jesús (Saint Theresa of the Child Jesus), El Turquillo, 1920
*Santiago (Saint James), Santiago-Talco, 1900
*Santo Niño (Holy Child), Monte Aplanado, 1830s
*Santo Niño de Atocha (Holy Child of Atocha), Buena Vista, 1876

THE PECOS AREA

*Nuestra Señora de Guadalupe (Our Lady of Guadalupe), Villanueva, 1818–1826

*Nuestra Señora de la Luz (Our Lady of Light), Cañoncito, late 1800s

*Nuestro Señor de Esquípulas (Our Lord of Esquípulas), Sena, 1908

*Sagrada Familia (Holy Family), Rowe, 1894

*San Isidro (Saint Isidore), Gonzales Ranch, 1932

*San Miguel del Vado (Saint Michael of Vado), Ribera, 1805+

GLOSSARY

Adobe. *Sp.*, a brick of sun-dried earth and straw used for building, with layers of mud added between each brick.

Adobero. *Sp.*, a wooden mold for making adobes.

Adze. A carpenter's cutting tool used for shaping wood.

Alabados. *Sp.*, hymns of praise.

Altar screen. A decorative screen or structure behind the altar in a church; retablo, reredos.

Anda. *Sp.*, a carrier upon which an image of the patron saint is placed before a procession. Also referred to as a *parihuela*.

Apse. A semicircular or polygonal projection of a church, generally at the east end.

Aranas. *Sp.*, spiders. A candelabra made from wood crossbars resembling spider legs, which holds rows of candles.

Articulated. Jointed, movable, as the arms of a carved santo.

Atrio. *Sp.*, a large walled yard enclosing a churchyard and cemetery.

Bulto. *Sp.*, a figure carved in the round, in the image of a saint, which has been gessoed and painted.

Buttress. A structure built against an exterior wall to support or reinforce it.

Byzantine style. Referring to an ornate, intricate style of architecture.

California mission style. In architecture, referring to a style which incorporates white walls and red tile roofs.

Campanas. *Sp.*, a term used for bells in New Mexico.

Camposanto. *Sp.*, graveyard within a churchyard.

Carpintero. *Sp.*, carpenter, woodworker.

Christ in the Tomb (El Santo Entierro). Usually a life-size representation of Christ in a wooden bier, generally with two handles on each end for carrying in processions.

Clerestory. The wall of a church rising above the roofs of the flanking aisles and containing windows for lighting the altar.

Cloister. A covered area surrounding the courtyard or patio of a convent.

Convento. *Sp.*, the official name for a Franciscan dwelling. A humble convent, as distinguished from a larger monastery.

Coping. A course of brick or stones covering the top of an adobe wall to prevent erosion.

Corbel. A short, carved timber supporting the weight of a roof beam.

Corinthian capital. In architecture, referring to the highly decorated top part of a pillar or column.

Crucero. *Sp.*, the front part of the church, forming the left and right parts of a cross.

Cruciform. Arranged in the shape of a cross.

Descansos. *Sp.*, wooden crosses indicating where a casket was placed on the ground while the pallbearers rested.

Double-hung windows. Windows which open from the top or the bottom and latch in the middle.

Fiscale. *Sp.*, an Indian official who assists in the functions of a pueblo church.

Funcion. *Sp.*, function, celebration; related to feast days.

Gable. A triangular wall enclosed by the sloping ends of a ridged roof.

Gesso. Crushed, ground gypsum mixed with water and animal glue and used as a painting base for retablos and bultos.

Gothic style. An architectural style reminiscent of fifteenth- century European architecture.

Hard-plaster. Plaster made from gypsum or cement and applied to adobe walls.

Latillas. *Sp.*, branches of aspen, or other trees from which the bark has been removed, used on ceilings between beams.

Louver. A series of sloping slats set in a window to provide air and light but to shed rainwater outward.

Lunette. In New Mexican folk art or furniture, a carved semicircular panel at the top of a retablo or altar screen; a shape representing baptism.

Mayordomo. *Sp.*, a member of the governing board of a parish or mission church; the boss of an acequia, or ditch.

Mission. An offshoot of a parish church, in the same area but distinguished from the parish by its size and location.

Mission revival. An architectural movement developed in Southern

California in late 1890, focusing on the rediscovery of (and style of) the California missions.

Morada. *Sp.*, a meeting house where the Penitente Brotherhood holds services.

Mud-plaster. Plaster made from mud and applied to exterior adobe walls.

Nave. The body of the church, as distinct from the sanctuary and the transept.

Nicho. *Sp.*, a shelf (niche) or cabinet of wood or tin which holds religious statues; an arched indentation in a wall for the same purpose.

Novena. *Sp.*, nine days of prayer to a specific saint.

Nuestro Padre Jesús Nazareno. *Sp.*, in santero art a life-size standing figure of Christ, generally with articulated hands and arms, usually clothed in a red robe and wearing a thorned crown.

Oratory. A small private chapel; *Sp.*, *oratorio.*

Parapet. A railing along the edge of a roof or balcony.

Parroquia. *Sp.*, the parish church, which is usually officially erected by the congregation and is self-supporting.

Penitente Brotherhood. A lay group of men who privately practice their religion and penance.

Pilaster. A rectangular support treated architecturally as a column, with a base, shaft, and capital.

Polychrome. Referring to carved wooden statues which have been gessoed and then painted in many colors, sometimes with the addition of gold leaf.

Portal. *Sp.*, a roofed entry way or porch.

Puddled adobe. Adobe mud which is poured into large molds to form walls as opposed to adobe bricks.

Pueblo revival. An architectural movement which revived the use of the earth forms and geometric designs of southwestern Indian dwellings.

Pueblo style. A style of architecture which uses pueblo dwellings as a prototype.

Reredos. An altar screen which contains several images of saints.

Retablo. *Sp.*, a hand-adzed wooden panel with an image of a saint painted on it, to which gesso has been applied.

Romanesque style. A style of European architecture based on the use of round arches and vaults.

Sacristy. A room generally adjacent to the sanctuary of a church, used for storage of sacred vessels and vestments and as a place where priests and assistants dress for services.

Sanctuary. The area in the church next to the altar occupied by the clergy, separated from the nave by a low railing.

Sangre de Cristo. *Sp.*, blood of Christ. A mountain range running from Santa Fe into Colorado called the Sierra Madre in the eighteenth century.

Santero. *Sp.*, painter and carver of images of saints.

Santo. *Sp.*, saint; image of a saint.

Southwest territorial style. An architectural style used from 1820–1860 which combined adobe, masonry construction with simplified wooden neoclassical detail.

Spanish revival. An eclectic architectural movement dating from about 1910 in which Mexican and Churrigueresque styles were used.

Spire. A tower tapering to a point.

Transept. The part of a cross-shaped church which is at right angles to the long, main section, or nave; either arm of this part, apart from the nave.

Transom. A crosspiece in a structure; a lintel; a horizontal crossbar across the top or middle of a window or the top of a door.

Transverse clerestory. Crossing from side to side; see clerestory.

Vaulted ceiling. An arched ceiling.

Viga. *Sp.*, the main supporting roof beams which are placed with ends projecting over opposite walls.

BIBLIOGRAPHY

Adams, Eleanor B., and Fray Angelico Chávez, eds. and trans. *The Missions of New Mexico 1776: A Description by Fray Francisco Atanasio Domínguez, with Other Contemporary Documents*. Albuquerque, N.M.: University of New Mexico Press, 1956.

Armstrong, Ruth. *New Mexico Magazine's Enchanted Trails*. Santa Fe, N.M.: New Mexico Magazine, 1980.

Boyd, E. *Popular Arts of Spanish New Mexico*. Santa Fe, N.M.: Museum of New Mexico Press, 1974.

Brown, Lorin W. *Hispano Folklife of New Mexico: The Lorin W. Brown Federal Writers' Project Manuscripts*. Albuquerque, N.M.: University of New Mexico Press, 1978.

Bullock, Alice. *Mountain Villages*. Santa Fe, N.M.: Sunstone Press, 1973.

Bunting, Bainbridge. *Early Architecture in New Mexico*. Albuquerque, N.M.: University of New Mexico Press, 1976.

Casey, Robert L. *Journey to the High Southwest*. Seattle, Wash.: Pacific Search Press, 1983.

Chilton, Lance, et al. *New Mexico: A New Guide to the Colorful State*. Albuquerque, N.M.: University of New Mexico Press, 1984.

Dickey, Roland F. *New Mexico Village Arts*. 1949. Reprint. Albuquerque, N.M.: University of New Mexico Press, 1990.

Ellis, Bruce T. *Bishop Lamy's Santa Fe Cathedral*. Albuquerque, N.M.: University of New Mexico Press, 1985.

Forrest, Earle R. *Missions and Pueblos of the Old Southwest*. Glorieta, N.M.: Rio Grande Press, 1883.

Fugate, Francis L. and Roberta B. *Roadside History of New Mexico*. Missoula, Mont.: Mountain Press Publishing Company, 1989.

Hall, Douglas Kent. *Frontier Spirit: Early Churches of the Southwest*. New York: Abbeville Press, 1990.

Hallenbeck, Cleve. *Spanish Missions of the Old Southwest*. New York: Doubleday, 1926.

Hazen-Hammond, Susan. *A Short History of Santa Fe*. San Francisco: Lexicos, 1988.

Jaramillo, Cleofas M. *Shadows of the Past*. Santa Fe, N.M.: Seton Village Press, 1941.

Kessel, John L. *The Missions of New Mexico Since 1776*. Albuquerque, N.M.: University of New Mexico Press, 1980.

Kubler, George. *The Religious Architecture of New Mexico in the Colonial Period and Since the American Occupation*. Albuquerque, N.M.: University of New Mexico Press, 1940.

Miller, Michael, and Kirk Gittings. *Monuments of Adobe: The Religious Architecture and Traditions of New Mexico*. Dallas: Taylor Press, 1991.

Prince, L. Bradford. *Spanish Mission Churches of New Mexico*. Cedar Rapids, Ia.: The Torch Press, 1915.

The Roads of New Mexico. Fredericksburg, Tex: Shearer Publishing, 1990.

Straw, Mary J. *Loretto: The Sisters and Their Santa Fe Chapel*. Santa Fe, N.M.: West America Publishing, 1983.

Warren, Nancy Hunter. *New Mexico Style: A Source Book of Traditional Architectural Details*. Santa Fe, N.M.: Museum of New Mexico Press, 1986.

——————. *Villages of Hispanic New Mexico*. Santa Fe, N.M.: School of American Research Press, 1987.

Weigle, Marta, ed. *Hispanic Villages of Northern New Mexico*. Santa Fe, N.M.: The Lightning Tree, 1975.

——————, and Peter White. *The Lore of New Mexico*. Albuquerque, N.M.: University of New Mexico Press, 1988.

Workers of the Writers' Program of the Work Projects Administration in the State of New Mexico, comps. *The WPA Guide to 1930s New Mexico*. Tucson, Ariz.: University of Arizona Press, 1989.

INDEX